Sex & Sense

A Contemporary Guide for Teenagers
Gary F. Kelly
Headmaster, The Clarkson School
and
Associate Dean of Students
Clarkson University
Potsdam, New York

BARRON'S

To my Betsy, who has enriched my life

All inquiries should be addressed to:
Barron's Educational Series, Inc.
250 Wireless Boulevard
Hauppauge, New York 11788

Library of Congress Catalog Card No. 92-43839
International Standard Book No. 0-8120-1446-4

Library of Congress Cataloging-in-Publication Data

Kelly, Gary F.
    Sex and sense : a contemporary guide for
teenagers / Gary F. Kelly.
        p. cm.
    Rev. ed. of : Learning about sex, 1986.
    Includes bibliographical references.
    ISBN 0-8120-1446-4
    1. Sex instruction for teenagers.
    2. Teenagers—Sexual behavior.
    3. Sexually transmitted diseases—Study and teaching.
        I. Kelly, Gary F. Learning about sex.   II. Title.

HQ35.K46   1992   92-43839
306.7'0835—dc20   CIP

PRINTED IN THE UNITED STATES OF AMERICA

3456   **CWI**   987654321

Contents

Preface

A great many things have changed since I wrote the original edition of this book in the mid-1970s. We were then in the midst of a shift in social attitudes about sex that sometimes has been called the "sexual revolution." People were talking and writing about sex more than ever before in our history, and were being more honest and open about their own sexual lives. Statistical studies of sexual behavior would suggest that people throughout North America were allowing themselves a somewhat greater degree of freedom with their sexual choices. However, even with all of the increased openness and freedom that the sexual revolution may have generated, human sexuality remained a complicated part of life. Making personal sexual decisions was still a difficult matter.

This book, originally titled *Learning About Sex*, was one of the first books for young people to be fully honest about many different aspects of sex. I was very gratified by the positive reception that it received. In subsequent revisions, I was able to use the suggestions of many readers to improve and refine the contents of the book even more. This is not to say that *Learning About Sex* was without critics. In fact, some groups and individuals were offended by the book's straightforward approach. Yet, as each criticism took me back to its pages to review what I had written, I continued to conclude that although the truth may be offensive to some, young people deserve only to be told the truth.

This new edition was prepared in a new time. Society has been wrestling with new problems such as H.I.V. and AIDS. Old concerns, such as sexual harassment, rape, and child sexual abuse, have received more open public discussion in recent years, and yet still have not been addressed effectively. Alternative sexual life-styles, including gay and lesbian sexual behaviors, have achieved a somewhat greater degree of legitimacy, and some laws and institutional policies now forbid discrimination on the basis of sexual orientation. At the same time, there is renewed emphasis on saying no to sex, and avoiding the physical and emotional risks that go with being sexually active. Confusion and conflicting attitudes about sex still exist, and understanding your own sexuality is still one of the most complicated parts of growing up and becoming an adult.

For these reasons, I am pleased to have had this opportunity to create a new book that is more in tune with the 1990s. It is still a very honest book. The facts about human sexuality really have not changed. However, the social climate in which we must make our sexual decisions, and the risks associated with those decisions, have indeed changed. This book recognizes and addresses these changes.

My own life also has changed a great deal since the first edition was published. I was younger then, and newly married. In the intervening years, Betsy and I have had two daughters who have become a central focus for our lives. So this new edition comes from a new personal perspective as well. I have become middle-aged, and I have parented my children as they grow toward maturity. I have answered their questions about sex as a parent. All of this time, I have continued to have the privilege of working with hundreds of teenagers who come to the school that I direct. I have watched the sex-related issues that concern them unfold. Some of those issues have remained consistent over the years, and some new ones have emerged. What is very clear to me is that young people today are still very interested in sexuality, curious about the spectrum of human sexual behaviors, wondering and worrying about how sex will fit into their lives, and anxious to understand themselves better.

I am particularly pleased that my older daughter Casey, a high school student, agreed to help me prepare this book. Although we certainly do not always see eye to eye on every issue, I respect her opinions and her insights about her peers, and know that she has been able to bring a young person's perceptions to our message. She is also a good writer, and working with her on this project has been fun.

As always, my wife Betsy has been a wonderful editor and sounding board for our work. She helped me think through most of the concepts I presented in the first edition, and has now helped Casey and me refine our ideas for this book. Some of our best ideas emerged from dinner table discussions that included our younger daughter Chelsea. I again am indebted to my family for their encouragement and tolerance for the hours of writing that sometimes take me away from them.

I am always interested in the reactions of readers to the following pages. Your comments and suggestions are useful for future revisions, and are always carefully considered. So please feel free to write and let me know your thoughts. I truly hope that this book will be of personal value and use to you.

Gary F. Kelly

1 Finding Your Personal Perspective on Sex

Sex is a complicated matter, and it seems to get more complicated every day. Sports stars, actors, and musicians admit publicly to having been infected by the AIDS virus through sexual activity. Politicians and judges debate whether abortion should continue to be available as a choice for pregnant women. Television airs hearings and trials about sexual harassment and rape. Movies, magazines, and music videos show plenty of skin and suggestive sexual scenes to turn us on. Other people tell us to say no to it all, and hope to turn us off. Understanding one's own sexuality and making sexual decisions in this kind of environment are not simple tasks. That is one of the reasons I decided to write this book.

Depending on the situation, I am known by several different titles, including sex educator, sex therapist, Associate Dean of Students at a university, and Headmaster of a school for talented high school students. Because of my involvement in these areas, I have worked with a number of local and national groups that help people understand their sexuality. It was because of these things that I was asked to write this book in the first place.

But for now, I would prefer that you forgot about my profes-

1

sional background because it is of secondary importance in the chapters that follow. What is most important is the fact that I am a sexual person, just as you are. We were born with biological sexuality—as male or female—but that is only the start. We also share a wide variety of sexual feelings. During my lifetime, I have often had to struggle to understand my own sexuality. By that, I mean that I have often been confused, afraid, guilty, or worried about my sexual feelings and sexual behaviors. At the same time, I have gradually accepted my sexual nature as a very positive and pleasurable part of my personality and of my life.

When I was experiencing confusion and worry about sex as a young man in my teens, I often wished I could talk with someone. There seemed to be no one with whom I could share these deepest feelings, and besides I was a rather shy person anyway. So, even though I joked around with other guys about sex and seemed pretty self-assured on the surface, I was quite alone as I tried to understand who I was as a sexual person. There were many things relating to sex about which I could not find much information, and I didn't always trust the stories that my friends had to offer.

Teenagers today certainly have access to a great deal more sex information than I did, but it is often presented in ways that are only arousing, confusing, or incomplete. There are still few opportunities to talk about the issues and think them through as individuals. That is another reason I wanted to write this book.

In part, this is the book I wished I could have had when I was young. It includes the topics I should have known more about, and that I should have thought very carefully about. With the help of my teenage daughter, and many other young people who have offered their suggestions, I have been able to craft a book that is appropriate for young people in the 1990s and the society in which we now live.

SOCIETY AND SEX

In different societies and times in history, there have been all sorts of attitudes and values about various sexual behaviors. What one culture believes to be unacceptable, immoral, or "sick," another culture may find perfectly acceptable. Human beings are social, and we tend to live in groups called societies. A particular society's attitudes about sex change with time as well. One way or another, we have to find ways of living with the values that are commonly accepted in our society, or suffer some consequences of being seen as rebellious and "antisocial."

North American societies did not deal very openly with human sexuality until the middle of this century. Sex was not considered to be a topic for open discussion, and young people usually were left to fend for themselves when it came to understanding their sexuality. Even married couples typically did not discuss sex very much or have a way to resolve the sexual problems that may have come along in their relationships. The various ways in which people expressed their sexuality were not given much open attention, and in fact were often considered too shocking even to mention.

There were a few writers and researchers who studied human sexuality, but their works were generally available only to physicians, or to the few people who were brave enough to get hold of their books through libraries or bookstores. In the late 1940s and early 1950s, a researcher by the name of Alfred Kinsey published studies on human sexual behavior that were based on personal interviews with thousands of people. These controversial books found their way to the general public, and opened up many new understandings about what people were actually doing sexually, even if they weren't talking much about it. Following this, other respected researchers began investigating sexuality more thoroughly. Gradually, a time of much greater openness and freedom with sex developed in the 1960s, 1970s, and early 1980s. This sometimes has been called the "sexual revolution."

Social Values Today

Plenty of people felt that the sexual revolution allowed people too much sexual freedom. As with any social movement, attitudes eventually swing back the other way. That has been happening with sexuality. We are now seeing a call for more caution and restraint with sexual activities. High numbers of teenage pregnancies, the appearance of AIDS, and the increase in other sexually transmitted diseases have caused some groups of people to say that sex should be avoided until one settles into a permanent relationship.

Things can get confusing when you try to figure out what your society believes about sex. In a large society such as ours, where there are a great many differences among people, there is little general agreement about how you are supposed to behave or what you are supposed to believe. In fact, there are many mixed messages that our society sends. As one teenager complained to me, "They tell us sex is dirty, and then say we ought to save it until we're married. Or they say sex is beautiful, but then won't talk to their kids about it. None of that makes much sense to me."

It is no wonder that we all get confused. On the one hand, sexual topics are everywhere. Almost every comedy show on television makes jokes about sex. Music is full of sexual references. Video rental stores often have adults-only sections where very explicit sexual movies may be chosen. Stories in the news cite statistics about the numbers of teenagers that are sexually active. It is pretty difficult not to get the impression that everybody's "doing it," or at least thinking seriously about it. Yet, on the other hand, lots of other people are warning that sex is dangerous, or wrong, or inappropriate until a particular time in life. It's hard to know what to believe.

Is Everybody Doing It?

One young woman said to me recently, "I'd like to know where all these people are who are having sex. Everybody talks as though it's going on all the time, but none of my friends are admitting to anything, and I think they're telling the truth. It's always everybody else. I'm beginning to wonder how much is really going on."

Studies to gather statistics on sexual behavior always run into problems. We never can be completely certain that people will tell the truth, especially if they cannot be absolutely certain that their responses will never be identified as theirs. Some people may feel embarrassed or guilty and not want to admit to the sexual things they have been doing. Others may want to brag about their sexual exploits and therefore exaggerate when they are asked questions about sexual behaviors. People who feel they are somehow different sexually may not feel ready to divulge their differences. Therefore, researchers tend to be cautious in their interpretations of statistics about sex.

The limited research that has been done over the past few decades does indicate some clear trends with sexual behavior. It is important to mention that these studies have focused almost exclusively on sexual intercourse (which is explained in more detail in Chapter 5). We do not have many up-to-date statistics on other forms of sexual behavior. These studies suggest that teenagers are indeed becoming involved with sexual intercourse much earlier than they did in the late 1940s and early 1950s. There was a particularly sharp increase during the late 1980s in teenage women who reported having had sexual intercourse. The best figures available now would indicate that among teenagers under the age of fifteen, somewhere between 5% and 17% of girls have experienced intercourse, and between 19% and 38% of boys have done so. This means that in these younger teen groups, many more people are not having sexual intercourse than those who are.

In the older teenage groups, the rate of sexual activity goes up. By the age of nineteen, about 68% of females and 77% of males indicate they have experienced sexual intercourse. How many times they have done so, or with how many different partners, seems to vary a great deal among individuals. Even these statistics tell us, however, that over one fourth of young people do not have intercourse during their teen years. So although the amount of sexual activity between boys and girls has certainly been on the increase in recent years, not everybody is "doing it."

What do these statistics mean for you? We always have to be careful how we interpret such figures. Such studies are one way of looking at social trends and making some sort of sense out of a mass of information. They do not say anything about what people should be doing, or what is "normal." They only describe roughly what is happening. What the statistics tell us is that some teenagers have had sexual intercourse, and some have not. They don't tell us why young people have made their decisions; whether they are happy with those decisions; or what sorts of consequences they may have experienced, either positive or negative, from their choices.

For me, these are the important issues to be considered when facing sexual decisions. Knowing how many people are having sex does not really tell me very much. Helping people to have accurate information about human sexuality, with which they may then begin to make their own sexual decisions, is far more important, and that is what this book is all about.

VALUES AND SEX

I do not think it possible to write a book about sex without having many of my own values, opinions, and points of view showing through. Perhaps if we just stuck to the facts about body functioning, less of myself would become a part of the discussion. But I believe it is important for every individual—young and old—to consider much more than just how his or her body functions in sexual ways. All of us must work to understand what role our sexuality is going to play in our lives: who we are as sexual people. And that means thinking and deciding about what we believe in, what kinds of people we want to be, how we are going to relate to other people, and what kinds of feelings we have. I hope that this book will help you to take a closer look at many of these things within yourself.

However, since many of my own values are going to be reflected in the pages ahead, I want you to know where I stand on many basic sexual issues. And I want you to understand that these are the values that have gradually come to have meaning and importance in *my* life. They have brought *me* happiness and satisfaction. That is not to say that they are the only "right" ways of thinking. You will have to sort through where you stand on these issues in your own way.

As you read about my values in the next few pages, you may see that you do not agree with some of them or you may realize that your parents would not agree with them. You may even decide that this is not the right book about sex for you. In any case, it is my hope that many people will keep reading and trying to decide where they stand. Even if you do not agree with an idea or value, it may be useful to bounce it around inside and thus clarify what your own ideas or values on the subject might be.

Here are some of the values about human sexuality that are important to me.

I believe that:

1. Our sexual feelings and behaviors are an important part of our lives with the potential for great pleasure and enjoyment. To have sexual feelings and fantasies is healthy and good. However, the potential for negative effects is also present in our sexual lives and that is why decisions regarding sex should be made with careful thought. The physical and emotional risks of sex must be considered thoroughly when making any sex-related decisions.
2. Each individual must spend time discovering how sexuality is going to fit into his or her life. That means eventually under standing one's own sexual feelings, sexual behaviors, and sexual preferences. It also means that in making decisions about sex, all of us must consider the sexual values of those people who are important to us, such as our parents, other relatives, and trusted friends. We should also consider the values we have learned from religion and education, and the values of our community and the larger society around us.
3. Each of us has a responsibility to show concern for other

people who come into our lives, whether it be in a sexual encounter or any other way. It is also important to have enough self-respect and self-esteem to show concern for ourselves in sexual decision making. Any sex that involves the exploitation or other hurting of someone else, or ourselves, surely loses some of its positive and pleasurable aspects.

4. People differ greatly in their preferences for various forms of sexual behavior. It is not always a simple matter to judge the "rightness" or "wrongness" of some of these behaviors. Instead, I hope that you can find the responsible and caring sexual life-style that is best for your own life—one that will provide great pleasure for everyone involved; lead to happiness and satisfaction; feel natural and spontaneous; and, of special importance, a sexual life-style that helps you to feel good about the person you are and the relationships you have.

How Do We Get There?

Did you ever stop to think how you have come to be the person you are? Why you have the values that you do? When we are born, our values are pretty simple and are based mostly on "creature comforts": loud noises are bad; being warmly cuddled is good; being hungry is bad; having bright things to look at is good. As we grow up, the picture gets far more complicated. People around us begin to teach us many more values.

As children, when we learn those lessons from other people well, we are praised and made to feel that we are good. When we do not do so well at showing that we have those values, we are made to feel guilty and that we are not so good. In this manner, we learn a variety of ways to see ourselves and the world around us.

For me, there was also a time when I was a teenager when I began gradually to question many of those values that had been taught to me. I was no longer sure they were all so right for my life.

When I expressed my doubts to my parents and teachers and a lot of other people, they sometimes would get angry with me. That would just make me more confused, and I often got angry too.

Yet, my questioning process had to continue, and it still continues today in my life. There are still issues and questions that are unresolved in my head. I still make mistakes. I still get confused. I still wonder and get scared about whether I am right or wrong. I still sometimes say or do the wrong things in my dealings with other people. But for now, I accept all of this as a part of my *life*. In fact, I am beginning to think that it all just means that I am *living*—thinking, feeling, sorting, and deciding—as I go. Maybe when I think I have "gotten it all together," it will just mean I've died a little. So I guess I hope I never get it there completely!

Where Do You Stand?

As I said before, I hope that one of the main uses of this book will be for you to take a close look at what you believe in. Probably on many issues, you're still thinking and wondering where you do stand. Good. I am hoping that you will take as long as you need to find the values and decisions that will feel right and good for you. Even if your mind is pretty settled on most issues, I also hope you will be open for change in the future, in case such a change would be best for your life.

For now, I would like to offer some questions about which I have discovered many young adults are thinking. I am certainly not asking you to answer the questions definitely and finally. Just see if you have thought about some of these issues and see just how clear your thinking is right now. They are purposely very open and general. Perhaps you will want to come back to these questions from time to time as you read this book and in the months ahead to see how your thoughts have changed or clarified themselves:

To what extent do you place other people's needs ahead of or behind your own needs?
What do you think about your own sexual feelings?

How important is masturbation in your life? How much meaning
do you place on it?

What kinds of things are especially sexually interesting to you?

How far will you go with other people to get whatever you want?

Do you think that the only proper place for sex is in a marriage
between a woman and man?

How do you feel about people whose sexual interests lie outside
the traditional social expectations?

How honest are you with other people about your feelings and
thoughts? How honest are you with yourself?

What is love to you, and what part does it play in your life?

What do the terms femininity and masculinity mean to you? How
do you express your femininity or masculinity to yourself and
others?

How much do you know about AIDS and how H.I.V. is transmitted
by sex?

Have you ever been taken advantage of, or exploited, in a sexual
way?

Where do you stand on using various methods of birth control?

What is your stand on abortion?

H.I.V./AIDS and Your Sexual Values

The disease AIDS, or acquired immunodeficiency syndrome,
is becoming more widespread all the time. Close to two million
people in the United States are believed to be carriers of H.I.V., the
virus that causes AIDS. Well over 200,000 people already have died
of AIDS. Sexual contact is one of the most common ways in which
H.I.V. is spread from person to person. Since there is no cure for
H.I.V. infection yet, it represents a dangerous threat. Indications are
that anyone who develops AIDS from the virus eventually will die
of it. This is a serious risk factor in sex, unlike anything human
beings have ever faced before. *Before you make any decision to
participate in sexual activity with someone else, be thoroughly
informed about H.I.V. and AIDS.* See Chapter 8 in this book.

About the Advice in This Book

You may not find as much direct advice in this book as you expected. Except for the clear-cut issues such as protecting your health and safety, and being respectfully considerate of yourself and others, I find it difficult to tell people exactly what they should or must do. This is disappointing to some, because many people are looking for others to tell them what to do.

I am not suggesting that I don't have strong opinions about the kinds of decisions that young people in our society make. In fact, I am alarmed that so many teenagers are choosing to become sexually active at such early ages. Not all of them end up being able to handle their involvements very well, and some suffer some negative consequences. Particularly scary is the fact that teenagers are among the fastest growing groups of people becoming infected with H.I.V. As a parent, and as an adult who has always worked with teens, I never want to see anyone hurt by their sexual decisions.

Realistically, though, I cannot assume that I know better how a person should live her or his life. And even if I did know best, people would not necessarily be prepared to listen to my advice. It might even push them to go in the completely opposite direction. It is important for me to accept that each of us has the responsibility and freedom to weigh decisions carefully in an individual way. It is important for me to respect and trust you enough to allow you to take responsibility for your own decisions and their consequences. Your life experiences will be different from mine; the choices and mistakes you make may be different from mine. That is a fact of living and growing.

This book will offer you the kind of factual information about human sexuality that can help you make your own decisions. It will provide you with some techniques for thinking through those decisions before you make them. It will caution you where caution is indicated. Along with the facts and bits of "advice" in this book, you surely will get plenty of ideas and suggestions from others. It is natural for people who care about you—your parents, brothers and sisters, friends, teachers, and others—to want you to be spared from hurt feelings, guilt, worry, unintended pregnancy, or illness. They sometimes want you to avoid making the same kinds of mistakes or poor decisions that they have made in the past. Listen carefully to the advice of these other people in your life. Weigh it, consider the quality of the person's life offering the advice, think and feel about it, examine it with the knowledge of who you are and what you want from your life.

What About Just Saying No to Sex?

When I was a teenager, about the only message we ever got about sex was this: DON'T. It wasn't always very clear exactly what we were not supposed to do. We were obviously not supposed to have sexual intercourse, because it could result in pregnancy, disease, and guilt. It also was considered to be wrong, although it was not always made clear why that was the case. It was difficult to get many answers about "how far" it would be all right to go sexually if you stopped short of intercourse. There were plenty of warnings about not allowing yourself to get into situations where anyone might get sexually aroused, because it made it more diffi- cult to stop before you "went too far." You were supposed to wait until you got married. This is not to say that everyone paid atten- tion to the rules. Teenagers did have premarital sexual intercourse, although not to the extent they do today. And they were involved in plenty of other sexual activities together.

The years of the sexual revolution changed some of this. Young people began to focus more on issues of personal freedom and responsibility in sexual matters. Many decided to use their own judgment when it came to sexual choices, and more couples began to choose sexual involvement. Some young people felt that the old prohibitions against having sex just did not fit them anymore.

As social values have begun to shift again, and with fears of H.I.V. infection and AIDS growing, there has been a renewed call for abstinence, or choosing not to have sex. Abstinence is sometimes called chastity, and if practiced for long periods of time is referred to as celibacy. Again, we find ourselves caught between conflicting sets of values. Some of the ideas about personal and sexual freedom are still around, and yet there are many messages calling for young people to abstain from sex.

There are good reasons for concerns about the increase in sexual activity among teens. The rate of unintended pregnancies has become extremely high, with about one in ten girls aged fifteen to nineteen becoming pregnant each year. Over 80% of those pregnancies are unplanned. The infection rates of most sexually transmitted diseases also have been on the rise, and the numbers of identified cases of H.I.V. infection and AIDS have been climbing at alarming rates. On top of all this, people have been talking more about the ways they have been emotionally hurt by their sexual encounters. It is not surprising that one reaction to the situation has been to call for an avoidance of sex altogether. Better safe than sorry.

However, there is another side to the story. Our sexual feelings are still strong. They still can have a very positive place in our lives. And as the statistics tell us, many young people are continuing to choose to have sex. This makes it all the more important that we are completely open and honest about human sexuality. If you are to make your decisions about sex responsibly, you will need all the facts. You also will need to think very carefully about each decision you make. Abstinence makes a lot of sense. It is worth considering very seriously these days. And until you feel very certain inside that you can choose a sexual experience freely, responsibly, and safely, it would at least be wise to say "Not now." I hope this book will give you the information and opportunity to think about decisions that will help clarify where you stand.

IN THE PAGES AHEAD

The main purpose of this book is to help you better understand yourself as a sexual person. That will mean learning more about the sex organs of your body and the ways in which they function. But that is only a part of the total picture. To understand your sexuality more completely, you also will need to take a closer look at your emotions or feelings and at your attitudes toward relationships with other people. It also will be important for you to learn more about the sex organs of the opposite sex. This book can help you accomplish all of these things.

Another important goal for this book is to emphasize that human sexuality is far more than our sex organs and what they can do with one another. Penises and vaginas are attached to real people, who have personalities, feelings, values, needs, fantasies, and so on. People relate to one another in many different ways, most of which do not even involve the sex organs. Our sexuality encompasses everything about us and how we perceive ourselves as females and males in our society. We bring that sexuality to every encounter with another person that we have, even if it is not "sexual" in any physical sense. Understanding what masculinity and femininity mean to us; sorting through how our loving feelings can influence our lives; and knowing what we want from our intimate relationships are as much a part of understanding our sexuality as learning about sex organs, pregnancy, and sexually transmitted diseases.

I have not tried to pull any punches in this book. I want to be honest and frank with you as you read on and learn more about sex. Nothing is meant to embarrass you or to make you uncomfortable.

The Words We Use To Talk About Sex

Talking about sex organs and activities can be a very private matter, and sometimes may be embarrassing. Perhaps out of that embarrassment, or perhaps because people are not always taught the "proper" terms for discussing sex, a great many slang terms have emerged. You probably have heard many of them. In earlier editions of this book, I included many of the slang terms to make sure everyone would understand what we were talking about. I also have discovered some problems with that approach. For one thing, whereas some people actually are more comfortable using slang than "proper" terms, others are embarrassed or offended by the slang terms. For another, there are so many slang terms being used, that I cannot possibly expect to include them all. I therefore have decided not to include slang terms in this edition.

You will have to decide what sexual words you feel are best for particular situations. When you're talking with a friend about sex, you may find it more comfortable to use slang terms than the more socially acceptable terms that I will be using in this book. Do try to keep in mind that slang terms may be offensive or even insulting to some individuals, and you will want to be considerate of their sensitivities. It may be particularly useful to learn the more socially acceptable terms so that you will be able to communicate with doctors, nurses, lawyers, or trusted adults who could help you in special situations.

As the reader of this book, you are in control of it. You may decide which areas you wish to concentrate on and which you wish to skip over or disagree with. I shall try to share my ideas as clearly and warmly as I can, and I hope that you will try to believe that I really do care about *you* as an individual and about your growth as a sexual person.

For Further Reading

Gale, Jay. *A Young Man's Guide to Sex.* Salt Lake City, Utah: Henry Holt, 1984.

Reinisch, June and Ruth Beasley. *The Kinsey Institute New Report on Sex: What You Must Know to be Sexually Literate.* New York: St. Martin's Press, 1990.

Voss, Jacqueline and Jay Gale. *A Young Woman's Guide to Sex.* Los Angeles: Price Stern Sloan, 1987.

2 Understanding Your Body

Think for a moment how your body looked when you were five or six years old. Sometime soon, you might even try to dig out some old photographs or home videos of yourself when you were younger. Perhaps you can find a picture of yourself in a swimsuit or maybe even with nothing on. What was your body like then? Chances are your body was mostly straight up and down—not many curves or bulges. It was also probably quite smooth, with the soft skin of a child and very little hair anywhere except on your head.

Think of how your body looks now. You probably often have a chance to see your naked body in a mirror. Sometime when you have the privacy you need, take a good close look at your body and think about the changes that have happened to it since you were five or six. What kinds of changes have occurred in you, and how far along you are with the changes, depend on your age, your rate of development, your sex, the characteristics you have inherited from your parents, and a variety of other factors. The chances are that you are "normal," regardless of what your body is like now.

Your growth and development are continuous throughout your lifetime. However, scientists who study human growth and development often find it convenient to divide the human life span into important events and stages such as: Birth, Infancy, Childhood, Puberty, Adolescence, Adulthood, Old Age, and Death. Regardless of which part of your life you are now living, you are, always have been, and always will be a sexual person. You may even remember the sexual feelings of your younger years and the curiosity you had concerning your sex organs. Your sexual feelings may be stronger now, and your curiosity may well be growing along with your sex organs. I feel as though I am still getting acquainted with the constant changing of my body, how it functions, and how it can give me pleasure.

Puberty is defined as that time in your life when your sex organs become capable of reproduction—producing another human being. That can happen at different ages for different people, but it is usually between the ages of ten and thirteen. It generally happens a little later for boys than for girls. There are many physical changes that occur in your body around this time. Once your body has reached puberty, you are considered to be an *adolescent.* The period of *adolescence* refers to that time when you are learning to be an adult. Many of us talk about adulthood, but few of us seem to understand fully what that means. Perhaps by the time you finish this book, you will know a bit more about what you think being an adult is all about. In any case, I never liked being labeled an "adolescent," so I shall avoid using that term in this book. You are a person, and this book can be useful to you at whatever age you wish to read it.

In the next few sections of this chapter, the changes of the male and female bodies are described, with special emphasis on the sex organs. I suggest that you read all of these sections thoroughly so that you get better acquainted with your own body as well as gain a fuller understanding of the bodies of others.

IF YOU ARE A MALE . . .

You have probably looked your body over carefully many times, and you may have seen the bodies of other boys (Figure 2.1). There certainly have been some important changes since you were five years old. I shall describe some of the changes that have probably already happened or that may happen to you soon. Looking at the drawings and diagrams in this chapter may help you to understand what is being discussed.

For one thing, you have grown taller. Around puberty, boys and girls go through several months of very rapid growth. Boys' shoulders begin to widen as they grow taller. Most boys have attained 98% of their final height by the age of eighteen. There is also a gradual increase in the amount of hair on the body. Darker, coarser hair appears under the arms, in the *pubic* area above and around your sex organs, and, eventually, on the arms, legs, chest, and face. How much hair you will have, what color it is, and where it is distributed depends mostly on characteristics you have inherited from your parents.

Another change you may have noticed is a deepening of the voice. As the larynx, or voice box, grows longer, the voice deepens. During the period when a boy's voice is changing, there may be some squeaking and cracking in the voice that some boys find embarrassing. Girls' voices become lower pitched also, but generally not as low as many boys'.

Penis and Testes

If you are a male, perhaps you have been especially curious about the changes that occur in your sex organs. Particularly noticeable is the increase in size of the penis and the testes. The penis becomes somewhat longer and thicker around the time of puberty and after. The two testes are located inside a pouch of skin called the *scrotum* or *scrotal sac.* Sometimes, the testes and scrotum are referred to as *testicles.* You will be able to feel that the

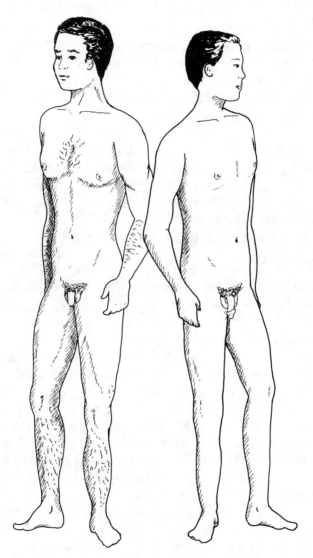

Figure 2.1

testes are larger and heavier than they were when you were a small child, and that they may be moved around slightly inside the scrotum.

Testicular self-examination

In the next few years, it will be important for you to learn how to examine your testes occasionally to check for any unusual lumps or bumps. The best time to do this is after a hot shower or bath, when the testes are hanging down from the body. Simply roll each testis between your fingers, and if you discover a small hard lump directly on the testis, report it to your doctor. You will feel tubes and other structures above the testes inside the scrotum, but these belong there. Lumps on the testes are not common, and may not be something to be very concerned about. However, if a lump is discovered, consult your doctor.

The skin of the penis and scrotum becomes darker as males grow and develop, and hair appears on the scrotum and base of the penis. As the testes get larger, the scrotal skin becomes somewhat wrinkled and has small bumps at the bases of the hairs. You probably have noticed that one testis hangs slightly lower than the other. This is true for most boys and men, and apparently has no particular significance.

The penis is a cylindrical shaft of tissues with a smooth, highly sensitive "head" or *glans*. When a boy is born, the head of the penis is covered by a fold of skin called the *foreskin* or prepuce. Sometimes, because of family tradition or religious custom, most of the foreskin is removed by a simple surgical procedure called *circumcision*. This would most often be done just after birth at the parents' request, before the baby boy is brought home from the hospital. It can be done, however, at any age if a doctor feels that it would be advisable. In recent years, there has been controversy in the medical profession about the advisability of circumcision. Some doctors feel it is completely unnecessary from a medical standpoint, whereas others feel that it helps prevent urinary infections in male infants and children. Fewer boys in the United States are circumcised now than once was the case. In many other cultures, circumcision is performed only rarely. If your penis is circumcised, you can see the head of the penis easily (Figure 2.2). With an uncircumcised penis, the foreskin must be pulled back for the head to be seen. Boys who are not circumcised should pull back the foreskin and wash the head of the penis often to prevent odor or mild infections from developing. The functioning of the penis seems to be the same whether or not it is circumcised.

Boys and men often worry about the size or shape of their penises and wonder if they are "normal" or not. In our society, it often seems that people believe the myth that the size of a man's penis has something to do with "how much of a man" he is. There is no truth to that belief at all. The size and shape of one's penis seems to be primarily the result of heredity. It does not seem to be related to the size of the person or any of his other body parts. Typically, the limp penis is between two and four inches in length after puberty, but normal boys and men may have penises smaller or larger than that. The shaft and head of the penis are found in a wide variety of widths and shapes, from thin and quite pointed to thick and very rounded. Some penises have a slight curve toward one side. Blood vessels are often visible beneath the skin of the penis.

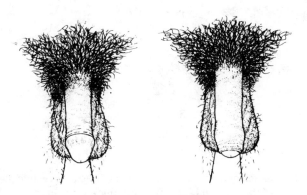

Figure 2.2 A circumcised penis (left) and an uncircumcised penis (right)

Boys usually notice during childhood that their penises some-times get stiffer and longer. This is called an *erection*. As you have probably already realized, erections happen when a boy becomes sexually excited or aroused. The ridge around the head of the penis is particularly sensitive, and stimulation of this ridge usually leads to sexual excitement and erection. There are a great many other things that can cause an erection, many of which have nothing to do with sex. Sometimes, for example, boys get erections when they are a little nervous or when they have to urinate badly.

Erection is the result of special nerve messages from the brain and spinal cord that cause blood to build up in the penis. There are three cylinders of spongy tissue in the shaft of the penis that become filled with blood. This causes it to become harder, thicker, and longer as it stands up and out from the body (Figure 2.3). When fully erect, most boys' penises are between five and six-and-a-half inches in length, although lengths considerably smaller and larger than those are perfectly normal as well. You may have noticed that the shaft of the erect penis is somewhat triangular in shape because of the three cylinders of spongy tissue inside. There is no bone inside the penis, as some people believe.

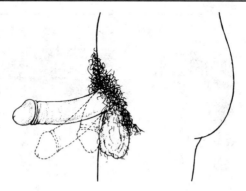

Figure 2.3   Erection of the penis. Because of built-up blood within the spongy tissues of the penis, it becomes longer, thicker, and harder, standing up and out from the body.

Erection occurs in most forms of sexual activity, but there are many forms of pleasurable bodily sharing in which erection need not take place. Kissing, hugging, and massaging each other can be very enjoyable forms of sharing, none of which depends on sexual arousal. See Chapter 5 for other forms of sexual sharing.

Functions of the Male Sex Organs

In the following discussion of male sex organ functions, it will help if you locate the organs on Figure 2.4, beginning with the testes.

Before a boy is born, his testes are located inside his body. During early embryonic life, they secrete chemicals that help create the male sex organs. Then, they remain relatively inactive until the boy approaches puberty. A few weeks before birth, the testes descend through a special tube (inguinal canal) into the scrotum. In a few boys, one or both of the testes may not come out into the scrotum, and sometimes medical attention is required during childhood to remedy the situation. As a boy reaches puberty, his testes have two very important functions:

1. To produce special chemicals called *hormones* that help control his growth and development as a man, including the body changes just discussed and his sexual feelings.
2. To produce the tiny, swimming units called *sperm* that are necessary for reproduction. Each sperm has a head and a tail (Figure 2.5). Sperm are so tiny that 120 million of them can be swimming in a small drop (1 ml) of fluid. They may only be observed through a microscope.

Each testis has within it tiny, tightly coiled tubules in which the sperm are produced. Laid end-to-end, the tubules from a single testis would stretch several hundred feet. The testes produce sperm from the time of puberty into old age, probably 500 million or *more each day!* As you may already know, the temperature of the human body is normally about 98.6° F. or 37° C. Sperm are best produced at temperatures three or four degrees lower than body

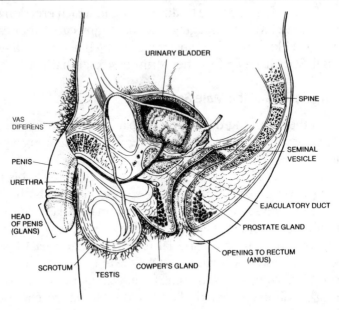

URINARY BLADDER

SPINE

VAS DIFERENS

SEMINAL VESICLE

PENIS

URETHRA

EJACULATORY DUCT

HEAD OF PENIS (GLANS)

PROSTATE GLAND

OPENING TO RECTUM (ANUS)

SCROTUM

COWPER'S GLAND

TESTIS

Figure 2.4 Sex and reproductive organs of the male: external and internal, side view.

temperature. This is the reason why the location of the testes in a special scrotal pouch is so ideal. The scrotum is supported by special muscles that can draw the testes up closer to the body or lower them farther away, thus regulating their temperature. For example, boys usually notice that when they are swimming or showering in cold water, their testes are tight up against their bodies. This keeps them warmer. In hotter surroundings, the testes are lowered away from the body to keep them slightly cooler.

In the head of each sperm is a set of twenty-three chromosomes, containing the genes that can pass characteristics on to our children. One of the functions of the male sex organs, then, is to transfer sperm to the female's body so that reproduction can take place. Chapter 9 includes further information on human repro-

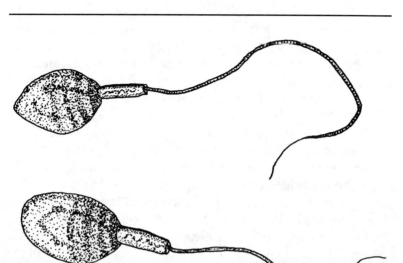

Figure 2.5 Two typical sperm produced by the testes of a human male, magnified here about 1500 times.

duction. We can now trace the pathway of the sperm to the outside of the body.

After the sperm are produced inside the tubules of the testes, they are slowly moved into other larger tubes where they may mature and grow for up to six weeks. During this time, the weaker sperm die and are absorbed by the linings of the tubes. Gradually, the remaining sperm are moved along through a duct which is about eighteen inches in length. There is one sperm duct, or *vas deferens,* from each testis, which conducts sperm up into the body to a *seminal vesicle*. The seminal vesicles produce a chemical that activates the tails of the sperm.

There are three glands that play a part in the safe passage of sperm to the outside of the body. One of these is the *prostate gland,* located just below the urinary bladder where urine is stored. The prostate produces fluids with which the sperm will be mixed before leaving the body. There are two glands, each about the size of a pea, located below the prostate gland. These *Cowper's glands* sometimes produce a fluid when a male is sexually excited. It is a clear, sticky liquid that lines the tube in the penis through which the sperm will leave the body. This tube is called the *urethra*. When a boy is or has recently been sexually excited, drops of this clear liquid may appear in the opening at the end of his penis. It is an alkaline substance that apparently neutralizes the acidity within the urethra, thus protecting the sperm.

The penis has some important functions for the body. It is through its urethra that urine is eliminated from the body and sperm eventually leave the body. It is an organ that is capable of giving males intense sexual pleasure. When a boy is sexually excited and his penis is erect, rubbing or other stimulation of the penis eventually leads to the pleasurable feeling of sexual climax or *orgasm*, accompanied by the spurting out of semen through the penis. This spurting is called *ejaculation*. There are special muscles in the body near the seminal vesicles that cause the semen to be ejaculated. Special muscles close off the bladder so that urine does not pass through the urethra during sexual activity.

At the time of ejaculation, the semen may just ooze out of the penis or spurt out with some force. How much semen is produced and with what force it is ejaculated depend on many factors, including the degree of sexual excitement and the amount of stimulation. The amount of semen may vary from a few drops to a teaspoonful or more. Before a boy's body begins making sperm and semen, it is possible for him to experience the pleasurable feeling of orgasm but no liquid is ejaculated. At various times in their lives, most boys occasionally experience orgasm and ejaculation while they are asleep. This is known as a *wet dream* or *nocturnal emission*. A wet dream can be surprising, even frightening, unless the boy is aware that it is a normal, healthy body activity.

Most boys know how sexual excitement makes them feel. There often is an intense desire to experience orgasm and ejaculation. Boys usually discover from their friends or through experimentation that by rubbing the penis—usually with the hands—orgasm can be produced. This is called *masturbation*. There is a whole section on masturbation in Chapter 3, pages – 65. Be sure to read it. Orgasm is also part of the sexual pleasure that can be shared in close relationships with other people. There is more about sexual sharing throughout this book.

IF YOU ARE A FEMALE . . .

You too have probably noticed some changes in your body, and in the bodies of other girls (Figure 2.7). Consult the drawings and diagrams in this section carefully and consider your own body. They can help you to understand some of what it means physically to be a girl and a woman.

Since you were five or six years old, you have grown taller. The period of rapid growth for many girls takes place a year or two earlier than for boys of the same age. Therefore, girls around the ages of ten or eleven often find themselves maturing physically before the boys in their age group. This is sometimes embarrassing for a girl—and for the boys—but perfectly normal. By the age of seventeen, most girls have attained 98% of their final height. As her body is getting taller, there is a widening of the pelvic or hip region. This widening may be of great importance in later life because a roomier area is being developed in which a baby may grow and develop before birth.

Body Development and Breasts

Pads of fat begin to develop under the skin in certain areas of the female's body as she matures, particularly on the hips, buttocks, and breasts. This results in the curvier body form of most women, as compared to the straighter body lines typical of men. At puberty, a girl's breasts also enlarge because of the addition of glandular tissue inside. When a woman gives birth to a baby, the glands in the breast will produce milk, which can be fed to the baby through the nipple. Milk is generally not produced by the breasts except after giving birth when the baby is nursing. As the breasts grow larger, so do the nipples and the darker area surrounding the nipple, called the *areola*.

Girls often have concerns and worries over the size and shape of their breasts or the color and shape of the nipples. The size of the breasts has nothing to do with "how much of a woman" she is, nor whether she will be able to breastfeed babies. Advertisers have capitalized on the anxieties of girls and women, offering a variety of exercise programs, bras and other equipment for making the breasts appear larger or "perfectly" shaped. In fact, breasts occur in a wide variety of sizes, shapes, and colors, all perfectly normal and healthy.

Breast self-examination

It is a good idea to learn how to examine your breasts, so that over a period of time you would be aware of any changes that might signal the presence of an infection or growth. When women reach their mid to late thirties, physicians are now recommending that they have *mammograms* on a regular basis. Mammography is a sensitive X-ray technique that can detect breast tumors even when they are very small. Although not all tumors are cancerous, breast cancer is one of the more common types of cancer in women, and the earlier it is detected, the better the chances of cure.

Women should learn from a physician or nurse how to best examine their own breasts, and then should do this examination themselves about once every month. The best time for the examination is about two weeks after the beginning of the last menstrual period. Just before or just after having a period, the breasts may have temporary natural lumps and swelling. Self-examination is demonstrated in Figure 2.6. First, inspect the breasts visually by looking in the mirror and raising your arms above your head. Look at them also as you lean forward toward the mirror. Check for any changes in the shape, skin texture, or nipple of either breast. During a bath or shower, while the skin is wet, the breasts may be examined with your hands. Use the hand from the opposite side of your body to examine each breast. Hold the fingers together, forming a flat surface, and begin by moving in circles around the outside of each breast. Gradually, you move inward with the circular motions until you have felt the entire breast. You should check for any unusual lumps, hard knots, or thickening of the breast tissue. The self exam should be done in both a lying down and upright position, because each position can help you feel the breast in different ways. Each nipple should be squeezed to see if there is any unusual discharge. Again, do not panic if you find some sort of lump or discharge, but it is always a good idea to report any area of concern to a medical person who can help evaluate it.

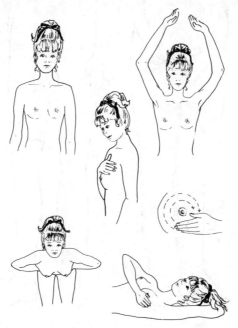

Figure 2.6 Breast self-examination.

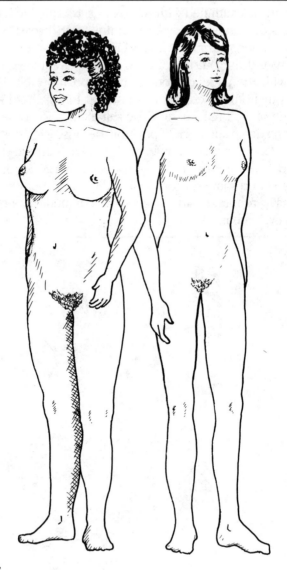

Figure 2.7

Bodily hair

The amount of hair on a girl's body increases also. Darker, coarser hair appears under the arms and in the pubic area around the external sex organs. Girls usually develop hair on their arms and legs, which some prefer to bleach or to remove by shaving or by using a hair-removing chemical cream. Our culture has created concern over bodily hair on females. Some girls are disturbed to have hairs appear on their faces, especially on the upper lip or chin. If temporary removal of these hairs through shaving or creams is unsatisfactory, a process called electrolysis can remove them for a longer period. A professional who has had special training in electrolysis should be consulted if one chooses to have hair removed in this way.

External Sex Organs of the Vulva

The changes in boys' sex organs are usually noticed more because their organs are easily observed. Nevertheless, important changes also occur in the external and internal sex organs of girls. All of their organs grow larger too.

A girl's external sex organs located between her legs are collectively called the *vulva* (Figure 2.8). Just above the opening between the two outer folds of skin in the vulva is a slightly rounded, padded area which becomes covered with hair as the girl enters puberty. This small "mound" of tissue is termed the *mons* (or *mons Veneris; mons pubis*). It is an area where the skin has many nerve endings and is therefore capable of adding to sexual excitement when rubbed or pressed.

The two folds of skin below the mons are called the major lips (or *labia majora*). These are sensitive structures also, and they serve as protective covers for the organs they enclose. If the major lips are parted, two smaller folds of skin are visible inside. These are the minor lips (or *labia minora*). They are highly sensitive to stimulation. During sexual excitement, the minor lips may flare out somewhat, showing the inner structures more clearly.

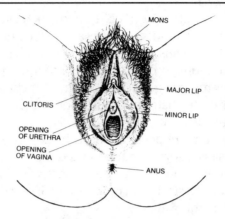

Figure 2.8 External sex and reproductive organs of the female: the vulva.

At the point where the two minor lips come together at the top, the *clitoris* is located. This is a small cylinder of tissue with a sensitive head or *glans*. Usually only the head of the clitoris is visible, while its shaft is covered by the upper folds of the minor lips. Although the entire clitoris is usually less than an inch in length, it may be considerably longer than an inch. It does not hang freely, but is attached along its underside. It contains two cylinders of spongy tissue inside and with stimulation it becomes erect—longer, thicker, and harder. The clitoris is a highly sexually excitable part of a girl's body.

Beneath the clitoris and between the minor lips, the opening of the urethra is visible. It is quite small and difficult to see. Urine passes from the bladder through the urethra and then leaves the body through this opening. Beneath the urethral opening is the opening to the vagina. The *vagina* is a muscular tube about three to four inches in length. It is capable of opening up when something is inserted into it, and during sexual excitement, it deepens slightly. The vagina can be a part of a variety of sexual activities, including receiving the erect male penis during *sexual intercourse*. More about that in Chapter 5.

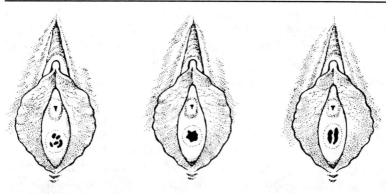

Figure 2.9 Three different types of hymens that may partially cover the opening of a girl's vagina.

In most girls, some tissue called the *hymen* partially covers the opening to the vagina. Hymens are observed in a variety of different shapes, some of which are shown in Figure 2.9. The hymen may be ruptured in many different ways. Sometimes, the hymen is broken by the penis during the first sexual intercourse. Insertion of other things (such as tampons) into the vagina or strenuous exercise may also break the hymen. When the hymen is first ruptured, there may be some slight pain and bleeding. This may be prevented by having a physician cut the tissue ahead of time, using a mild local anesthetic.

In many cultures, the presence of the intact hymen has been a sign that the girl is a *virgin,* a person who has never had sexual intercourse. This is obviously not a reliable sign, since the hymen may be ruptured by other means, or—in the case of a particularly flexible hymen—it may not be broken during intercourse at all. Therefore, the presence or absence of a hymen signifies nothing. It is not an indication to doctors that a girl has been sexually active or not.

Many girls and women discover that pleasurable feelings may be produced by rubbing areas in the vulva with the hands or stimulating the sex organs in other ways. Sexually stimulating oneself is called *masturbation*, discussed more completely in Chapter 3, pages 63–65. Be certain to read that section. After a certain time of such stimulation, the pleasurable release of sexual climax or orgasm may be reached. Orgasm is also part of the sexual pleasure which can be shared with other people.

One of the most important signs that a girl has reached puberty is the beginning of *menstruation* (having her "period"). This involves the loss of some fluid, mixed with a small amount of blood, through the vagina about once a month. The first time this happens, a girl may be surprised or frightened unless she has been fully informed about why menstruation occurs and that it is a normal, healthy function of the female body. In the following two sections, we shall discuss a girl's sex and reproductive organs in

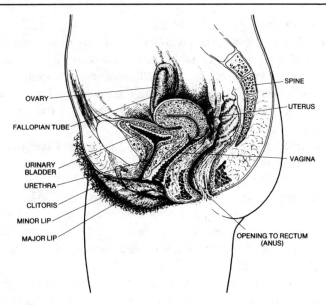

Figure 2.10 Sex and reproductive organs of the female: external and internal, side view.

more detail, including the importance of the menstrual cycle in human reproduction. Menstruation is only a part of that cycle.

Inner Sex Organs of the Female

We have already discussed the external sex organs of a girl. You will recall that inside the minor lips, in the area of the vulva, there was an opening to the vagina. By examining Figure 2.10, you will note that the vagina leads upward into the body to the *uterus,* or womb, inside of which a baby can develop. Near the uterus, there are two ovaries, each having a narrow *fallopian tube* that leads to the uterus. These organs are essential to human reproduction.

Each ovary is about an inch in length. As a girl reaches puberty, her two ovaries have two very important functions:

1. To produce hormones that help control her growth and development as a woman, including the body changes just discussed and her sexual feelings. These special chemical substances also help control the menstrual cycle.

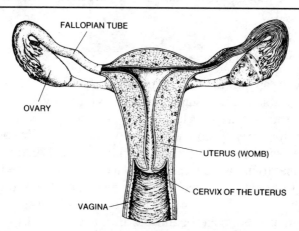

Figure 2.11   The female reproductive system: front view, isolated from the body.

2. To produce the tiny *eggs*, or *ova*, necessary for reproduction. The ova produced by human females are about $\frac{1}{175}$ inch in diameter, much larger than the male's sperm. It is when a sperm from a male joins with the female's ovum that a new human being begins to develop (also see Chapter 9).

At puberty, each ovary contains about 10,000 tiny cells that can become eggs. During a woman's lifetime, only 400 to 500 of them will actually "ripen" to become ova and then be released from the ovaries. The fallopian tubes, sometimes called *oviducts*, carry the ova that are released to the uterus, a journey of about four inches which takes about two days.

The uterus is about the size of a doubled fist and has somewhat the shape of a pear. It has very thick, muscular walls and a hollow interior. The tip of the uterus that opens into the vagina is called the cervix. The uterus is sometimes a site of cancer in women, and a Pap Test—described on page 234—can detect trouble before it gets serious. The Pap Test should be part of a regular physical examination for all women. Figure 2.11 will help you understand the relative position of these organs and their activities as you read on.

The Menstrual Cycle

If you can now identify the internal organs of the woman, you should be able to understand the changes that they undergo each month—the menstrual cycle. This cycle begins at puberty (usually between the ages of ten and fourteen), and generally continues until the woman is in her middle to late forties. When a woman then ceases to menstruate, she is said to have experienced menopause. Some people refer to this time as her "change of life," although really not very much else changes. During the years before menstruation has begun and after it has ended, the female is unable to bear children.

The number of days in one complete menstrual cycle varies with different individuals. For teenage girls, it is most often thirty

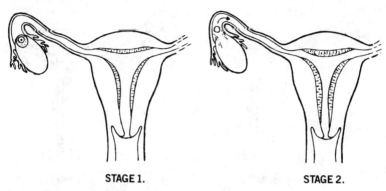

STAGE 1.   STAGE 2.

Figure 2.12 The menstrual cycle.

or thirty-one days in length. As girls enter their twenties, the amount of time often decreases, so that the average menstrual cycle takes about twenty-eight days. What actually happens is that the ovaries and uterus prepare for pregnancy each month. If pregnancy does not occur, the prepared areas are shed from the body, and the cycle starts all over again. The main stages of the cycle are described below. (See Figures 2.12 and 2.13.)

1. In one of the ovaries, one of the eggs ripens and becomes larger, ready to produce a new human being if it is joined by a male sperm. In the meantime, there is a thickening of the inner lining of the uterus. Blood and other materials begin to build up in the lining so that if a developing baby, or *fetus,* is to grow there, it will have a nourishing environment to keep it alive.

2. As the uterine lining continues to thicken and prepare for pregnancy, the ovum (egg) breaks through the outer wall of the ovary. This release of the egg is called *ovulation.*

3. The egg is released into the fallopian tube, which is lined with microscopic hairlike projections called cilia. These move the ovum along toward the uterus for about two days. If the egg is to develop into a fetus, it must be joined by a sperm

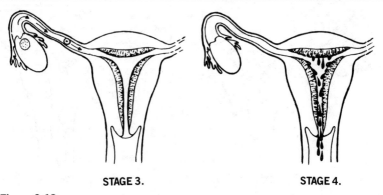

STAGE 3.   **STAGE 4.**

Figure 2.13

while it is in the tube. As the ovum moves along, the uterus becomes especially ready to nourish a fetus. Its linings are very thickened and filled with blood.

4. If the egg does not meet with the sperm by the time it reaches the uterus, it apparently disintegrates. Then, the extra material which has thickened the lining of the uterus is no longer needed, and it gradually begins to deteriorate. Eventually, some of this fluid and blood leaves the body through the vagina. This is menstruation, and it usually lasts from three to seven days. The cycle then continues, with the ripening of another egg and another build-up of nourishment in the uterine lining.

As the extra lining of the uterus is deteriorating, particularly just before menstruation, some girls and women experience unpleasant symptoms. These can include fatigue, headaches, abdominal cramps, tenderness in the breasts, an increase in pimples, and moodiness. In women where these symptoms are quite strong, the condition is called premenstrual syndrome, or PMS for short. Some women are able to tolerate the symptoms better than others. Medications of various sorts may be prescribed by a physician to prevent or relieve more severe complaints.

The fluid and blood that flow out of the vagina during menstruation must be absorbed in some way so that clothing will not be stained. There are two types of absorbent aids that girls may purchase. One is an absorbent *sanitary pad* that is placed over the vaginal opening. These pads come in a variety of sizes and absorbencies to suit the needs of different girls. The pads are held in place by a strip of adhesive that sticks to the underpants. Another aid that many girls find convenient and easy to use is the *tampon*. This is a cylinder of absorbent material that is inserted directly into the vagina. Tampons generally do not cause discomfort, and they do not in any way stretch or damage the vagina. If a girl has difficulty inserting tampons because of her hymen, she should start with a small sized type, slowly widening the opening of the hymen. Tampons should be changed frequently so that bacteria do not build up on them in the vagina. This can cause infections, including a very serious illness called toxic shock syndrome. The printed instructions included with tampon packages give specific advice on prevention of this infection.

Despite the myths of former times, physicians seem to agree that girls and women need not limit any of their activities while they are menstruating. There is no harm at all in bathing and showering, shampooing the hair, swimming, being physically active in sports, engaging in sexual activity, or doing anything else during menstruation. Girls should avoid using menstruation as an excuse for not participating in everyday activities unless a physician has advised them of some special condition about which they should be cautious.

In learning more about human reproduction, described in more detail in Chapter 9, it is important to understand the menstrual cycle. There is further information about the cycle in that chapter.

GROWTH AND GROWING

We have dealt with some of the major physical changes that occur as we grow toward adulthood, especially the changes in our sex organs. For most of us, our physical growth is unavoidable. With a reasonably balanced diet, protection from the elements, and freedom from serious disease, the human body develops and grows older in a continual state of balanced change.

Think of the people in your life whom you have known for several years. Think of how they have changed. They have grown older and their bodies have changed in a variety of ways, just as yours has. But there is more to living than just growing older. We grow inside, too. It is easy to see others and ourselves growing older, but quite a different matter to get in touch with the inner growth that is also happening. Yet, to live fully and happily, it is necessary to keep in touch with that growth as closely as possible.

One of the most important areas of inner growth is our *emotions*. As most people enter their teenage years, they are beginning to get in touch with more intense feelings than they knew in childhood. They may begin having strong loving feelings for other individuals, and these loving feelings not only bring pleasure, but confusion and hurt as well. They may begin feeling depression, guilt, boredom, and fear more than when they were children. They may also feel new joys and satisfactions in their lives. Getting acquainted with all of these new intensities of feeling is part of what inner growing is all about. It is important to realize also that even when an emotion is not very pleasant, it still may be worth feeling. It may be a part of our growth as a person. We often learn to escape from our "bad" feelings as quickly as possible, when there may be real value in allowing ourselves to feel them for awhile.

Another part of our inner growth is understanding our relationships with other people. Our attitudes toward many things may change with time, if we allow ourselves to be open to such change. We need always to keep in touch with what kinds of responsibilities we feel toward others and the extent to which we need other people in our lives. Whenever we set our minds on opinions or values that *cannot* be changed no matter what, we have stifled our own growth.

Time Out

Sometime soon, try to take time for the following activities. I have suggested them to many young people, and they often report back that the exercises helped to put them in touch with themselves and their inner growth.

1. *Body awareness*

    Find a comfortable and quiet place where you can relax. Close your eyes, and allow your hands to move lightly over your face. Touch and *really* feel your eyelids, nose, lips, ears, and neck. Pay attention to the warmth and texture of your skin. Blow your warm breath on your hands and feel the warmth. Move your fingers slowly through your hair, noting its texture and "feel." Try to become aware of the rest of your body also. Where do you feel tension? What are the areas of your body which feel the pressure of touch?

2. *Alone time*

    We live in hectic times. It always seems there is something to do or somewhere to go, leaving very little time for ourselves. I would like you to set aside some time just to be by yourself. An hour or more would be best. If you have brothers or sisters who are noisy, or always around, go for a walk outdoors. Most important of all, spend this time *thinking about yourself and letting yourself have inner feelings.* If you get around to thinking about your sexuality, you might want to consider the following questions:

    (a) How does your body seem to compare with the bodies of others your own age?

    (b) What things about your body are you most satisfied with? Most dissatisfied with?

    (c) Have you had any worries about your sex organs or sexual activity lately? Think them through and consider seeking out someone else to talk with. (See Chapter 7.)

    (d) Does your interest in sex seem much stronger than it used to be? Most people sometimes worry that they are thinking about sex too much, even though their great interest in sex is perfectly normal. Have you been worrying about that?

3. *Sharing*

If you have a friend whom you trust and can talk to, perhaps you could try discussing some of the above questions with him or her. The friend may then be willing to share some thoughts and concerns with you. Don't be upset, however, by differing point of view. Perhaps they will just make you think.

For Further Reading

Bell, Ruth. *Changing Bodies, Changing Lives*. Westminster, Maryland: Random House, 1987.

Madaras, Linda. *What's Happening to My Body?: For Boys*. New York: New Market Press, 1988

— —. *What's Happening to My Body?: For Girls*. New York: New Market Press, 1988

McCoy, Kathy and Charles Wibbelsman. *The New Teenage Body Book*. Los Angeles: Price Stern Sloan, 1987.

3 Finding Your Sexuality

The last chapter dealt mostly with the physical part of our sexuality—the sex organs. I keep trying to emphasize that there is much more to your sexuality than just your sex organs. This chapter will begin to explore how your sexuality is part of your entire life, and the changing concepts of femininity and masculinity; and it will discuss in more detail how our bodies respond sexually. These are important considerations in understanding your own sexuality.

SEXUALITY AS A LIFELONG PROCESS

Our sexuality is part of our lives from the moment we are born, and is partly formed even before birth. It includes not only our sex organs, but all of the emotions, thoughts and fantasies, ways of behaving, and sexual interests that make up our personalities. Our sexuality includes the ways in which we see ourselves as girls and boys and women and men, and how we live out our sex roles in our society.

When it comes to sexuality as part of the human personality, each of us is very much an individual. We each have unique personalities, and just as no two bodies or personalities are exactly alike, the sexualities of different people are also different. The unique features of each person's sexuality develop over an entire lifetime. As we grow up, we gradually learn about our sexual feelings and needs, and find a place for them in our lives. That process continues until we die. Our sexuality grows and changes as we develop and age. Even into very old age, sexuality remains a part of being human.

Emerging Sexual Feelings

Children often have sexual feelings and can even experience orgasm. At puberty and during our teenage years, most of us experience our sexual feelings with greater intensity. In thinking about what I would write in this section, I realized how difficult it is to describe sexual feelings. For the most part, they can only be understood when they are felt. The term "sex drive" is often used to describe our desire for sexual stimulation and release. Sometime in late childhood and as we grow toward adulthood, there is usually an increase in this desire, which is partly the result of increased amounts of sex hormones produced by the testes and ovaries.

At first, the deepening interest in sex may produce a vague inner tension, a longing for something that is not clearly defined. Eventually—and this occurs at different ages and rates for different individuals—the sensations become more definitely located in our sex organs. Sometimes, this longing is referred to in slang as being "horny."

There are differences among people in their degree of interest in sex. For example, some boys and girls become sexually aroused very easily and desire orgasm often. Teenagers often feel these needs rather intensely. On the other hand, some young people do not find themselves particularly interested in sex. These differences are perfectly normal.

As people grow older and go through different periods of their lives, there may be changes in the intensity of their sexual interests, and those changes may occur in either direction. In old age, there may be some gradual decline in the desire for sexual release. That does not mean, however, that older people enjoy their sexual feelings and activities any less.

It has traditionally been believed that boys have a stronger desire for sexual activity than girls, and research has shown that boys in general seem to have more frequent orgasms during their teenage years than girls. There are, of course, many individual exceptions to these statistical trends.

There is disagreement among professionals as to how much of our sexual interest is due to physical causes in our bodies and how much is due to learning. For example, some say that any differences in sexual interest between teenage boys and girls are attributable to built-in organic differences. Others insist that boys are simply encouraged more to explore their sexual feelings at earlier ages, whereas most girls are not. Perhaps if such differences really do exist, they are explainable as a combined result of organic factors *and* learning. Only further investigation will clarify the answer. The important thing is to become comfortable with whatever degree of sexual interest that seems to be a part of your personality.

As we "awaken" more fully to our sexual feelings, we often begin to feel some guilt. Hopefully, as you read through this book, your increased understanding of your own sexual feelings will help to lessen unnecessary guilt for your life.

How Our Bodies Respond Sexually

To understand your sexuality more fully, it is essential to know how your body responds when it is aroused by sexual feelings. There was little reliable scientific information available about sexual response until the 1960s, when researchers began to study the body's responses to sexual stimulation. Dr. William Masters and Virginia Johnson published a book titled *Human*

Sexual Response, based on ten years of research into how the human body reacts during masturbation and intercourse. Sensitive medical devices were used to measure and record the many changes that occurred in people's bodies, and it was found that both males and females go through predictable stages of sexual response, summarized below.

For easier understanding of sexual response, it is helpful to know that sexual response involves some major changes within the body. First, there is a build-up of muscular tension, and the flow of blood is routed into the area of the sex organs. This is the "turn-on" phase of sexual response. After a while, orgasm may occur, which acts as a trigger for the release of the built-up tension. Gradually, the body then returns to its unexcited state, and blood flow returns to its usual patterns. In their study, Masters and Johnson found it useful to divide this series of bodily responses into four distinct stages: Excitement, Plateau, Orgasm (or climax), and Resolution. It should be understood, however, that there are no distinct divisions between these stages. Figure 3.1 graphically shows the four stages.

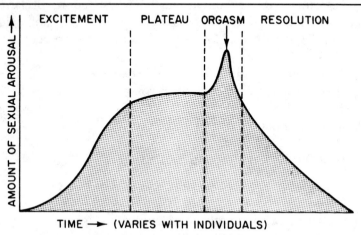

Figure 3.1 The Stages of Human Sexual Response.

Now we shall consider what happens during each stage.

1. *Excitement*
   In slang, this phase is often referred to as getting "turned on." There is an increase in muscular tension throughout the body, and the nipples of both males and females may become harder and erect. Many women and men experience a "blushing" of the skin on the chest, abdomen, and neck, known as the "sex flush." The heart begins to beat faster and blood pressure goes up somewhat.

   In males, the most obvious sign of sexual excitement is erection of the penis. In females, the inner walls of the vagina undergo a "sweating" reaction and become somewhat wet, while the width and length of the vagina increase about 25%. The clitoris of the female also becomes erect. All of these reactions are the result of the increased flow of blood into the pelvic area.

2. *Plateau*
   During this stage, the changes begun during excitement become more intense. Muscular tension in the body increases, along with heart rate and blood pressure. The rate of breathing has usually increased by this stage too. The reddening of the sex flush may appear now if it has not before.

   In males, the testes are pulled up closer to the body in the scrotum, and the head of the penis becomes more swollen with blood than before. A few drops of the clear secretion from Cowper's glands may appear at the tip of the penis. In females, the clitoris pulls back under the folds of skin that cover its shaft, and the amount of lubrication in the vagina may increase. Both the scrotum and vulval lips swell somewhat with the increased blood flow into their tissues.

3. *Orgasm or climax*
   This is one of the most difficult parts of human sexual response to describe. Although orgasm lasts only a few seconds, it is one of the most intensely pleasurable experiences

in human sensation. During orgasm, the muscular tension that has built up during excitement and plateau is released.

At the time of orgasm, the body has reached a peak of tension. In the male, muscles at the base of the penis in the ejaculatory duct contract to push semen out of the penis—ejaculation. The first three or four contractions are the strongest and occur slightly less than a second apart. Females also experience such contractions in the vagina, and may sometimes even emit a small amount of fluid that has collected there. While these pleasurable contractions are occurring, the body muscles of both males and females may be involuntarily contracting—often quite strongly. The entire pelvic area may undergo thrusting movements. The individual may gasp or cry out. A pleasant "tickling" sensation is usually felt throughout the body. People report that they have different types of orgasms at different times, some being more powerful and pleasurable than others. Some people also enjoy sexual activity without reaching orgasm at all.

4. *Resolution*

Immediately following orgasm, the body begins to return to its state before sexual excitement began. The muscles become very relaxed within about five minutes, while heart rate, blood pressure, and breathing all return to their typical rates. Gradually, the sex flush disappears and the nipples lose their erection.

In males, the penis loses about half of its erect size within a short period of time. Then, more gradually, the penis returns to its nonexcited size and limpness. The testes relax and move slightly down from the body again. Males also go through a period known as the *refractory period*, during which they cannot reach orgasm again. This period may be very brief (a few minutes) or last longer (hours), depending on the male's age, degree of sexual stimulation, and individual sexual needs.

In females, resolution includes the return of the clitoris to its regular position almost immediately and the return of the vagina to its unstimulated size within ten or fifteen minutes. However, most females do not seem to have a refractory period, and some may reach orgasm more than once during a single sexual experience.

Individual Differences in Sexual Response

Whenever an individual is sexually aroused and is stimulated to reach orgasm, he or she goes through the stages described above. The stages occur regardless of the means of sexual stimulation: masturbation, intercourse, or other shared physical contact. There may be some variations in the details of the stages, especially in females. The most pronounced differences, however, are in the amount of time that various individuals take for the sexual response to occur. It is possible for some individuals to move through the entire process—from excitement to resolution—in a very few minutes, whereas others may spend an hour or more. How long sexual response takes depends on many circumstances, including what the person has learned regarding his or her own sexual pleasure.

Sex and Aging

Young people often have difficulty realizing that adults—even older adults—have sexual needs. We do not lose our ability to feel sexually or to enjoy those feelings at any particular age. Our bodies may age and change, our degree of interest in sex may change, but we are sexual people all of our lives. We may experience sexual joys and sexual worries at any age.

As people get older, their degree of interest in sex may decrease gradually and physical illness may hinder their enjoyment of sex. However, most people retain their potential to enjoy sexual feelings, including touching and caressing, even into their seventies, eighties or beyond. Getting acquainted with the changes of our sexuality is a lifetime proposition.

BECOMING WOMEN AND MEN

Becoming an adult woman or man amounts to more than having your body become fully grown and sexually mature. Becoming a male or female in the first place is a complicated process in itself. That process is put into motion at the time of conception, when a sperm enters an egg. It is at this time that the genetic sex of the human embryo is determined. This is further explained in Chapter 9.

Becoming a Girl or a Boy

It is the genetic combination in the cells of the embryo that determine whether testes or ovaries develop during the first two months of embryonic development. Research into the development of male and female characteristics has shown that in order for an embryo to become male, special chemicals called hormones must be produced in the embryo. Otherwise, the embryo automatically will become female.

In an embryo that has male genes, the testes form during the sixth week of development. These tiny testes then produce two hormones that turn embryonic tissues into a penis, scrotum, and internal male sex organs, while preventing the development of female sex organs. If the embryo has female genes, the ovaries appear by the twelfth week of development, but they do not secrete any hormones. The embryonic tissues automatically develop a clitoris, vagina, vulva, and internal female sex organs.

So it is during fetal life, before birth, that these clear physical differences in sex organs between females and males are established. At birth, everyone is interested in whether the baby will be a boy or girl. As soon as the baby's sex is established, social influences begin to shape how the child is viewed by others. Every society has certain roles and expectations for boys and girls, and as they are growing up, the "rules" for being a girl or a boy are learned by everyone.

Masculinity and Femininity

Just how different are males and females? Or are they more alike than they are different? These are questions that continue to be debated by social scientists around the world. Some have suggested that the same biological factors that shape whether a child is a girl or a boy also build in some differences in personality and behavior. Others insist that the main differences are only in the sex organs, and that personality factors are shaped more by how boys and girls are treated as they are being raised.

At this point, it seems most likely that certain conditions of being male or female are established during fetal development, before the child is born, but that learning then plays an important role in determining what a girl or boy is like as she or he grows. Masculinity and femininity are the names we give to the personality factors and behaviors that we tend to associate with being male or female.

For many years, the roles that were expected of men and women in our society were very rigid. Table I summarizes some of the stereotyped views of men and women that persist even today. Some people still hold tightly to these stereotypes, whereas others are adopting a more flexible viewpoint.

TABLE I
THE TRADITIONAL STEREOTYPES
OF WOMEN AND MEN

WOMEN	MEN
Emotional and flighty; cry often and worry easily	Unemotional and stable; control their feelings and worries
Delicate and somewhat physically weak; tire easily and cannot stand prolonged physical exertion	Muscular and strong; have much stamina to withstand physical exertion

Content with household tasks such as cooking, cleaning, sewing, and caring for children	Enjoy the pressures and demands of business and earning money
Shy and retiring	Aggressive and forward-moving
Should not become sexually involved unless married	Expected to become active sexually at an earlier age and to "sow a few wild oats"
Tender and caring for children and others more helpless than themselves	Tend to be colder and less tolerant toward children and others
Quite easily swayed by the suggestions of others; tend to be followers	More independent and levelheaded; not easily swayed by others; tend toward leadership
Have less self-confidence and self-esteem	Confident and proud; stand up for themselves
Concerned with people and their feelings	Concerned with impersonal objects and mechanical gadgets
Argue about petty matters; enjoy gossip with other women	Concentrate on important issues of politics and society; do not gossip
Are not expected to initiate sexual experiences	Are expected to be aggressive sexually and initiate sexual contact
Become sexually aroused only by the romantic and loving aspects of a relationship; are not interested in nudity or thinking about sex	Are not interested in romance; become sexually aroused by nudity and thinking about sexual acts
Only have loving or sexual feelings for men	Only have loving or sexual feelings for women

The list could go on and on. You may think that some of the characteristics are exaggerated, but such attitudes have been very commonly held by a great many people. In some ways, it was probably easier to become a man or woman a few years back because the rules for your behavior were so specifically spelled out! However, I am very glad that you will have the chance to think through very carefully what kind of woman or man you want to be and then have a better opportunity to make the decisions and take the directions that will get you there.

The fact of the matter is that nobody is *all* "masculine" or *all* "feminine." Every boy and girl, woman and man, has the potential for a wide range of behaviors and traits, some of which society may have considered to be more feminine, whereas others are considered to be more masculine. Girls can be aggressive and enjoy competitive sports. Boys may be emotionally sensitive and cry easily.

As we grow and develop, we gradually get a sense of ourselves as male, female, or perhaps some combination of the two. This sense of our maleness or femaleness has been called *gender identity*.

Part of finding and understanding your own sexuality must be deciding what masculinity and femininity mean to you. There are many influences on your life that must be considered: parents, peers, religious teachings, and your community. But most importantly, you must stay in touch with your own feelings about your own womanhood or manhood, your own gender identity. At the end of this chapter, you will find some questions and activities that may help you sort through these areas of your life.

Jason, Lisa, Scott, and Julie

What is expected of men and women today? What does it mean to be "masculine" or "feminine" now? I had the privilege of discussing these questions with four high school students, and I am now bringing portions of that discussion to you. At the time of our meeting, Jason and Lisa were high school seniors and seventeen years old. Scott and Julie were juniors, aged seventeen and sixteen respectively. I think that what they have to say is quite representative of current values on masculinity and femininity:

Lisa: Sometimes, I don't know how to act anymore. I think it used to be easier when girls were supposed to act certain ways and boys were too.

Julie: But so much of that was phony, Lisa. What about girls like me? I don't particularly care for dresses, and I'm good at playing tennis. Before, I would have been a real outcast unless I dressed up in frilly clothes and let boys win when I played tennis with them. You know, girls were supposed to be dainty and not very competitive.

Jason: That probably wasn't true for all boys. If a guy feels all right about himself, then it shouldn't matter if he gets beat by a girl in tennis or not.

Julie: Well, I was exaggerating. But the point is, now we are being encouraged to be whatever kind of girl—or person—we are.

Scott: But I kind of like girls who are a little shy, and I like feeling strong and protective toward them. If I ever do get married, I sure don't want to do much of the cooking and cleaning either.

Julie: So you would be willing to let your wife do all the dirty work!

Lisa: It isn't dirty work if you like it. I like to feel protected by a boy, and I like to cook. I'm not very competitive when it comes to sports.

Julie: Do you think you would always be happy doing things for a guy and having him always be the winner in everything?

Gary: I'm not certain that was quite what Lisa was saying, Julie.

Lisa: No, it wasn't. I enjoy cooking, and I'm good at it. That's something I can share with a husband and other people, and feel good about myself for. He can be good at different things and feel good about himself too.

Gary: I guess that is the real key to a good relationship between two people. The both of you being able to feel good about yourselves and each other.

Jason: I don't think that I could feel very good about a girl who was only interested in cooking, sewing, and other traditional "girl things." I want to be with someone who is involved in life—in the world. That way, we both have lives of our own and interesting things to talk about with one another.

Scott: Then isn't that the kind of girl you should look for? But other guys may want to look for other types of girls.

Julie: Getting back to what you were saying a minute ago,
           Scott. Did you mean that you wouldn't help out around
           the house?

Scott: Not necessarily. That would depend on a lot of things. If
           I was the only one working at a job, then probably my
           wife should take care of the household stuff. If she
           worked too, then we could either hire someone to help
           out around the house, or we would share the work.
           Only I don't like to cook or clean.

Gary: Again, maybe the important thing would be to have the
           kind of communication that would permit you to work
           it out together so you both are reasonably satisfied.

Julie: But there have to be compromises, and we sometimes
           may have to do some types of work we don't like.

Gary: True. We're getting a bit away from talking about femi-
           ninity and masculinity, though. Things have been
           changing with regard to how girls and women are
           "supposed" to be. How about the ways boys and men
           are "supposed" to be.

Jason: Same thing. I don't think boys have to put on the big act
           anymore. You know—tough, silent, unemotional, al-
           ways in control. I cry sometimes and I don't have to feel
           ashamed that crying is "unmanly." I like art and some
           classical music, and I don't like football. But now, it's
           okay for me to be that way. I know I'm still a boy, and
           that's the main thing.

Julie: There are still some things that are considered femi-
           nine. Things like sewing and ballet, for example. That's
           stupid, because it might save men a lot of money and
           trouble if they could sew, and ballet dancers have to be
           very strong, athletic, and competitive.

Scott: A lot of it seems to be in the way you're brought up.

Gary: Yes, how are we taught to be masculine or feminine
           from the time we are very young?

Lisa: Girls are given dolls and toy stoves to play with, and boys are given baseball gloves and toy guns.

Jason: Boys aren't allowed to cry as much as girls, and they are encouraged to be braver about everything.

Julie: If I have children, I don't see any reason to raise the boys any differently from the girls. I'll let them have whatever interests they seem to develop. I just want them to be good people who will care about other people—not robots who are playing some games of being boys and girls.

Lisa: But everyone learns some of the more traditional boy and girl roles.

Gary: And those roles may be very much a part of the persons we are. There is nothing wrong with roles as long as they are a real part of you—not just some act to please someone else—and as long as they feel right and comfortable for your life.

Scott: How do you know if something is really part of you now or whether it is just something you do to fit in? Sometimes when I'm doing something the way a guy is expected to do . . .

Gary: For example?

Scott: . . . like playing hockey. Well, I sometimes feel right in the middle of a game as if I don't even want to be doing it. It's as if the only reason I'm involved is to show that I am a guy.

Jason: I think what it really means to be a man is to know yourself and what you want for your life, then to carry through with it. And it doesn't matter if you play hockey or sew or tiptoe through the tulips with pink satin slippers!

Julie: That goes for being a woman, too. Women can like hockey, and you shouldn't have to have big breasts or go to bed with guys to prove that you're a woman.

Scott: That part also applies to guys. You don't have to have a lot of sexual experience to be a guy. Sometimes I think that we're still expected to know everything about sex so we can teach girls, but it shouldn't be that way. Everybody should learn about sex, but what you do with it is still up to you.

These young people expressed some important ideas concerning trends in today's society. There is general agreement that people deserve the same opportunities for personal fulfillment and satisfaction, regardless of their sex. The central issue is not whether men should open doors for women, whether wives should have jobs while their husbands stay home with the kids, or whether women should be interested in sports. Instead it is the freedom for each of us—both women and men—to be the full person he or she is capable of being.

Social and Political Movements About Gender

Societies often regulate what people are allowed to do based on their sex, or gender. In the United States, it was not until 1920 that women were even allowed to vote. Men are still required to register for possible military service when they reach the age of eighteen, whereas women are not. There have been various political movements designed to change social attitudes and laws that seem to discriminate against women or men.

One such movement that has been part of our society for many years is the feminist movement. *Feminists* are people—both female and male—who reject the idea that either sex is in any way inferior to the other. They advocate equality of women and men socially, politically, legally, and in the job market. They work to see that men and women are treated equally, trying to assure, for example, that both sexes are paid the same for the same sorts of work. Feminists are not man-haters, nor are they only women. They simply believe that no one should suffer discrimination because of gender.

Recently, some people have been reacting to the roles that they feel have made life more difficult for men. This has led to what is sometimes called the *men's movement*. Some men have been meeting in groups to discuss male roles, their own emotions and concerns, and the directions they want for their lives. Many men want to be able to express their full range of emotions more readily, and want to break out of the roles that assume they must devote more energy to careers than they do their families.

There is a great deal of misunderstanding about feminism and men's groups. People sometimes joke about them, or are angered by them. Again, these social and political movements are made up of people who want to see women and men accepted as individuals, and treated as equals. They recognize that there are all sorts of differences among human beings, some that are related to gender and many that are not. Human differences may be appreciated, even celebrated, and need not become reasons for unfair treatment.

The In-between Gender Identities

If we imagine masculine gender identity to represent one end of a range, with feminine gender identity at the other end, we would find the majority of men placing themselves toward the masculine end, and the majority of women placing themselves toward the feminine end. However, there are some individuals who cross the boundaries that are typically considered appropriate for men and women. Some people have gender identities that are not consistent with their physical sex, and their behaviors may reflect this in-between gender identity.

Cross-Dressing

Some people enjoy dressing in clothes of the opposite sex. This may be done as a gag, such as for a Halloween costume, or may have more sexual implications. Some people cross-dress occasionally for fun; they are then said to be "in drag." There are some people who get sexual satisfaction from dressing in clothes usually worn by members of the opposite sex, or who simply feel more like themselves in such clothes. These people are called *transvestites*. It is typical to equate transvestism with homosexuality. In fact, most cross-dressers are heterosexual persons. Although transvestism is harmless to others, there are laws that permit the arrest and prosecution of transvestites in some cities and states.

Transsexualism

Transsexualism should not be confused with homosexuality. The transsexual is a person who feels that he or she has the personality of the opposite sex. Transsexuals often feel from the time they are very young as if they are trapped in the wrong body, and this may lead to frustration and depression. With the true transsexual, counseling or psychotherapy aimed at helping the individual to accept the body he or she was born with is not generally effective. It is sometimes advisable for transsexuals to undergo treatment at medical centers where their bodies may gradually be changed by hormonal and surgical treatment to resemble a body of the opposite sex. Several thousand people in the United States have undergone surgery to alter their bodies and sex organs in this way.

As we may see, femininity and masculinity, and how people feel about themselves as men, women, or some identity in-between the two, are very complicated matters. People's gender identity, or sense of themselves, may not always be consistent with the sex organs they have, or with the expectations of their society. This is another example of how each of us has a sexual nature uniquely our own.

SEXUAL INDIVIDUALITY

You have noticed how the kinds of food you like and dislike are different from some of those that other people like and dislike. Some people relish foods such as mushrooms, caviar, wines, and spinach; others find them unpleasant to the taste. Some people feel very hungry most of the time, whereas others need to eat very little. It is much the same with the sexual appetites of human beings. What is a sexual turn-on for one individual may be a real turn-off for another. Although some of us are interested in sex most of the time, others seldom feel such interest.

Each of us has his or her own very unique set of sexual interests, needs, feelings, fantasies, and preferences. I refer to this as *sexual individuality*.

It may be too early for you to know fully what kinds of things you will find sexually interesting, but wherever you stand now, it is important to understand the varieties of sexual behavior that human beings experience.

What is "Normal"?

It seems that we spend a lot of our time wondering whether or not we are "normal." Are we too tall? too short? too thin? too fat? Boys wonder if their penises are normal; girls wonder if their breasts are normal. We wonder about our sexual thoughts and feelings too.

Professionals who work with people have difficulty defining what is normal and what is not. One way to do it is by gathering statistics: if a large number of people fit a particular pattern, then it is "normal." But there are some flaws in that approach. Assume that a study is done that shows that 98% of fifteen-year-olds in the United States like pizza. Would that mean that the "abnormal" few who do not like pizza are sick? When it comes to sexual behavior in our society, there are still some fairly strong ideas about what patterns may be considered "normal" and "healthy." However, the facts are that millions of people simply do not fit these patterns and yet continue to live happy, productive lives. We must begin to realize fully that each of us has his or her own legitimate set of sexual attitudes and feelings.

Most professionals in the field of human sexuality today seem to agree on one thing: that an individual's sexual orientations and

behaviors need not be considered unhealthy unless they are
causing physical or emotional harm to that individual or to others.
At various times in our lives, most of us experience some concern
or worry about our sexuality. That does not mean that our sexual
feelings or attitudes have made us "sick." It simply means that it
might be a good idea to talk over our concerns with a friend or
counselor (see pages 142—145).

A small percentage of people do adopt types of sexual behavior that are dangerous or hurtful to others. These are discussed
in more detail in Chapters 7 and 10 of this book. Such individuals
may require special professional help.

Sexual Orientation and Preference

Most people find themselves inclined toward being sexually
interested in some specific other people. That may be because of
the physical characteristics of these people, and/or the qualities of
their personalities. You may find yourself particularly attracted to
females, or to males. This general sexual inclination is sometimes
called a person's *sexual orientation* or *preference*. People also
develop preferences for particular kinds of sexual activities. Even
though people may become sexually involved with other persons
or activities that do not necessarily completely fit their basic
orientations or preferences, the basic interests tend to persist over
time.

We do not yet fully understand how our individual sexual
orientations and preferences develop. There may even be some
influences on our sexual feelings before we are born. For the most
part, however, it seems that our sexual interests and preferences
are discovered over a long period of time. During childhood and
adolescence, many parts of our sexual nature become well-estab-
lished in our personalities. Once established, many of those parts
stick with us for a lifetime, others change.

It is important to emphasize, however, that we may also exert
control over our sexual impulses. Sometimes in films and litera-
ture, people are portrayed as being at the mercy of their sexual

feelings, being led into wild sexual encounters by uncontrollable instincts. That view is inaccurate. Human beings are capable of making responsible decisions about what they want to do sexually. Our sexual feelings are very strong and influential in our lives, but well within whatever controls we want to place on them. The point is, then, that we are all capable of finding happiness and satisfaction in our sexuality, and it may take some work to accomplish that.

Another important thing to remember is the changing nature of our sexuality. Over the years, our preferences for certain foods may change. Similarly—although perhaps not as simply—our values and preferences for certain sexual things may change too, depending on our circumstances, relationships with others, and our own changing needs. This does not mean that if there is something about our sexuality we do not like, that it will just pass away in time or that we can force it to change. If you are dissatisfied with parts of your sexuality, it may be the right time to think and talk about them and to understand them more fully. In time, you might even become more accepting of the sexual person you are.

Curiosity About the Body and Sex

From the time we are very young, most of us are interested in what the nude bodies of others look like. We are curious to see their sex organs, not only those of the opposite sex, but others of our own. That curiosity is natural and normal. It is especially predictable in a culture that does not encourage nudity. The bodies depicted in most pictures tend to be what our society considers to be attractive or "perfect." Some people are curious to know what everyday people look like. For some people, however, this natural curiosity is carried to extremes that offend others. They invade the privacy of others by peeking through windows, hoping to catch a glimpse of someone in the nude. This may be done by groups of young people for fun or by an individual who feels a desperate need to do so. If a person is caught peering in someone's window, they could be subject to arrest and prosecution. As much as many of us might enjoy looking at other's bodies, it should never be done in a manner that could be frightening or embarrassing to others or in violation of their right to privacy.

SEXUAL BEHAVIORS AND PERSONAL RESPONSIBILITY

Growing out of their sexual interests, orientations, and preferences, people eventually begin to become involved in sexual activities or behaviors. A behavior is something that we do. Naturally, a significant part of human sexuality is the sexual things that people do, and there is a wide range of these sexual behaviors.

An important aspect of understanding our sexuality is knowing where our sexual feelings fit into our lives and how we express them. Through the years, the various forms of sexual behavior have been judged by many different moral codes. In other words, different societies have judged them to be right or wrong.

We live in times where there are great differences of opinion concerning the rightness or wrongness of various sexual activities. There are those who believe that any form of sexual behavior is right as long as it feels good, those who believe that the only permissible or right form of sex is intercourse after marriage, and those who fall somewhere in between those two extremes. Again, you will have to think carefully about where you fit in that spectrum of beliefs, now and in the future.

We have to give these questions our careful attention before we are faced with sexual decisions. To be a responsible person, we have to take time to weigh our needs and desires with the teachings of those who are important in our lives. Then we can at least begin to make decisions that are based on thought and planning. Yet, as always, our decisions are our own.

Masturbation

You will recall that masturbation refers to self-stimulation of the sex organs to produce sexual arousal and, usually, orgasm.

Many young people first get in touch with their sexual feelings through masturbation. Studies have shown that nearly all boys and the majority of girls masturbate quite regularly. A boy most often masturbates by grasping his penis with his hand and stroking it or by rubbing his penis against some object. A girl usually masturbates by stroking her clitoris or the surrounding area or by massaging the entire area of vulva. Many boys, girls, men, and women experiment with a great variety of ways to masturbate. Most people fantasize (daydream) about things that they find sexually exciting while they masturbate.

Unfortunately, masturbation is not often talked about and consequently many misunderstandings have developed about it. For many years, some adults—thinking masturbation to be dangerous to health—told youngsters wild stories about the frightening consequences of masturbation. These myths included claims that masturbation would cause pimples, insanity, mental retardation, and physical weakness! Other myths, perhaps less frightening but just as false, persist today. If your parents or others tell you these things, it is not because they are trying to be cruel. They are simply reflecting what they have been taught. These include the ideas that masturbation will weaken you so you will not be as successful in athletic endeavors and that "too much" masturbation will cause a boy to run out of sperm so he will not be able to produce children. All are totally untrue. Another myth is that only youngsters masturbate, and when they establish mature relationships, masturbation ceases. The fact is, most adults continue masturbating occasionally throughout their lives, and often into old age.

In years past, people were so convinced that masturbation was bad and dangerous, parents would take extreme measures to prevent their children from masturbating. Devices were designed to prevent youngsters from touching their sex organs—including metal mitts to put on their hands at bedtime and various sorts of belts (chastity belts) that were placed over their sex organs.

Fortunately, times have changed. Most physicians and other professionals agree that masturbation is a normal and effective outlet for sexual tension. There is also no such thing as "too much" masturbation, nor will anything bad happen to your body if you do not masturbate. Some people masturbate only a few times per year, whereas others masturbate several times a day. Some people choose not to masturbate at all. Different individuals have different sexual needs. Apparently there is no harm to mind or body, regardless of the frequency with which masturbation is practiced. Contrary to popular opinion, there are also no laws that prohibit masturbation in private.

Some of the negative attitudes toward masturbation still exist, however. As a result, some individuals are still left with some guilt or anxiety each time they masturbate. Of course, over a period of time, such feelings may build up to some fairly negative attitudes about oneself. If you have been troubled by such feelings, perhaps it would help to talk them out with someone you can trust. See "Finding a Counselor," pages 142—145.

Again, it will be up to you to decide how masturbation is to fit—or not fit—into your life. It is okay not to masturbate as well. Some religious teachings hold that masturbation is immoral and should not be practiced. If these beliefs are a part of your background, you will want to give them appropriate consideration.

Many professionals today believe that masturbation has benefits. They feel that the practice helps young people to understand and become better acquainted with their sexual feelings. Additionally, it is felt that masturbation may serve as a good substitute for sex with another person before the young man or woman is emotionally ready for that step in a relationship. If boys use masturbation to learn how to prolong the amount of time it takes to reach orgasm—instead of hurrying to finish—they may be learning how to be better sexual partners for future relationships. Girls may learn how to reach orgasm through masturbation, and that ability may be transferred to satisfying sexual contacts later.

Sexual Thoughts, Fantasies, and Pictures

At one point or another in their lives, most people worry that they are thinking about sex too much. They may experience fantasies (daydreams) or dreams about sex during sleep, some of which may include pretty wild activities. The important thing to keep in mind is that most people think and fantasize about sex. That is nothing to worry about or apologize for. Our fantasies—even our wildest ones—cannot hurt anyone unless we act on them or become overly obsessed with them. It is our actions for which we must be responsible and about which decisions must be made. At times, our fantasies and thoughts may give us clues about what we find sexually interesting, but they are just portions of our imagination—nothing to be feared. Of course, it is important to be able to distinguish fantasy from reality.

Some individuals enjoy looking at pictures of people who are nude or engaged in sexual acts. Such materials are available in magazines, movie films, videos, and other forms and are often referred to as *pornography.* That term means that the material is of a sexual nature that may be sexually arousing for some people. Others find such materials offensive and obscene and feel that they should not be made available to anyone. There have been many laws passed and court decisions made about pornography, but as things now stand, many sexually oriented pictures and gadgets are available to those who want to pay for them.

There have been two national commissions that have studied pornography, but neither has been able to clearly define what its harmful or positive effects might be. Some citizen groups are calling for bans on sexually explicit materials. Some people feel that pornography offers a distorted view of sexual relations because of its emphasis on the purely physical aspects of sex. Others feel that most pornography reflects a rather negative view of women, and is demeaning to them. Pornography that depicts children and other minors involved in sex is illegal.

It should be kept in mind that pornography does not adequately portray what really goes on between most people sexually, nor does it emphasize the importance of a healthy, communicative relationship as a basis for sexual sharing. If such material is the only outlet for sexual feelings, to the exclusion of meaningful relationships with other people, then the individual may want to examine his or her needs more closely to determine if the pictures have become a kind of escape.

Other Sexual Preferences

When it comes to sexual "turn-ons"—things that are sexually arousing and interesting—human beings are remarkable for their diversity. Many people associate various odors or objects with sexual excitement, such as perfumes, or soft blankets, or leather objects. There is no particular harm in finding such things sexually arousing as long as they do not detract from the sexual sharing that may be a part of close loving relationships.

Although there may be some roughness and strenuous physical activity in many sexual encounters, some people have come to associate discomfort, some degree of pain, or domination and submissiveness with sexual arousal. This sexual orientation is termed *sadomasochism,* or *S and M.* Another variation on the S and M theme is *bondage,* which involves tying a person during sex or binding particular parts of the body to create pressure. The obvious dangers of such behaviors lie in possible unintentional physical injury that could occur, or in an exploitative relationship where one person forces a partner into acts in which she or he does not want to participate.

There are a number of other human sexual preferences. However, there are few reliable statistics to tell us just how common these preferences are. Many forms of sexual behavior are not considered acceptable to many people in our society, including some of the preferences discussed in this chapter. Those forms of behavior that are generally considered to be unhealthy and harmful to others are discussed in Chapters 7 and 10. It should be remembered that any form of sexual behavior may have its unhealthy aspects unless it is understood, accepted, and responsibly enjoyed by the individual and is not harmful or guilt-producing to that individual or others.

DECISION-MAKING AND YOUR SEXUALITY

Several times already in this book, it has been stated that you will have to figure out what you want for your life—now and in the future. In other words, you are the one who is going to have to make the decisions of what you want to do with your sexuality. There will be plenty of people who will try to persuade you one way or another, but the final decision always rests with you. That is a fact of life that can even be scary at times because it also means that we have to take responsibility for the consequences of our decisions. There is a great variety of sexual things that people can do and feel. This book examines the varieties of sexual inclinations and behaviors that human beings may have. It explores the possible consequences of sexual behavior, both positive and negative. I hope you will consider this information carefully as you make the sexual decisions for your life.

WHERE ARE YOU NOW? A QUESTIONNAIRE

The following questionnaire is meant for *your own use*. Do not write answers in the book for others to see. You should not be asked to share answers with anyone else—even anonymously. If you choose to talk over your answers with a trusted friend, that, of course, is up to you.

How would you answer the following questions? Think about your answers carefully. There are no "right" or "wrong" answers, no "normal" or "abnormal" answers—just *your* answers.

Yes ☐ No ☐ Have you sometimes worried that you think or fantasize too much about sex?

Yes ☐ No ☐ Do you think that your sexual fantasies are "wild"?

Yes ☐ No ☐ Do you enjoy looking at pictures or movies of nude people or sexy scenes?

Yes ☐ No ☐ Have you ever felt sexually aroused by another person of your own sex?

Yes ☐ No ☐ Have you ever participated in sex play with a person of your own sex?

Yes ☐ No ☐ If so, did you feel upset or guilty about it?

Yes ☐ No ☐ Do you often think about having a sexual experience with someone of the opposite sex?

Yes ☐ No ☐ Have you ever participated in sex play with a person of the opposite sex?

Yes ☐ No ☐ If so, did you feel upset or guilty about it?

Yes ☐ No ☐ For the most part, are you happy with your sexuality?

At this point in your life, what things interest you most sexually? _____

At this point in your life, what sexual preferences are most difficult for you to understand and identify with? _____
_____

What would you *most* like to change about your body or sexual preferences? _____
_____

What would you *least* like to change about your body or sexual preferences? _____

Who Are You as a Sexual Person?

The following exercises can help you clarify and understand your own sexuality if you do them with careful thought. Most of them could also be used with a friend or in a group of people who would like to talk over these issues together.

1. *Masculine—Feminine*
   (a) Examine the following list of qualities and check which

you want for yourself as a man or woman (add words of your own if you wish):

honest	physically strong	responsible
brave	dominating	emotional
athletic	delicate	persuasive
loving	intelligent	protective
competitive	successful	shy
gentle	submissive	reliable
sensitive	manipulative	flighty
aggressive	thoughtful	sincere
considerate	confident	sexy

(b) Now, read through the list of qualities again and pick out those that have been traditionally considered masculine and those traditionally considered feminine. Make two separate lists on a sheet of paper. Some words may appear on both lists or neither. Again, include any words you have added to the list.

(c) Finally, note where the qualities you checked for yourself in (a) fall in your two lists. Think about them. This should help to show how your goals for your own masculinity or femininity relate to traditional ideas about men and women, as you view them.

2. *You and your parents*

Spend some time thinking about your parents' ideas of what is masculine and feminine: what they consider appropriate for women and men. How are your ideas the same and how do they differ? Perhaps you will want to talk over these thoughts with your parents.

3. *How do you react?*

Read each of the following statements and think about them. How do you react to them? Do you agree or disagree, and how strongly? Perhaps you could discuss them in a classroom or other situation:

(a) A newspaper story reported that a Superintendent of Schools in a Minnesota community directed his teachers and counselors "to teach such values as preservation of the family unit with the feminine role of wife, mother and homemaker and masculine role of guide, protector and provider."

(b) A group of boys in a gym class discovered another boy masturbating in a locker room bathroom. He was obviously embarrassed, but the boys who discovered him continued to joke about the incident for weeks after.

4. *Making decisions*

(a) You may already have made some decisions about sex for your life. For example, you may have decided whether or not you want to masturbate or engage in sexual activity with someone. Are you still satisfied with your decision(s)? What things did you consider in making your decision? Do you ever consider re-thinking the decision and changing your mind? Why? Would your parents be happy with your decision?

(b) Next time you are facing any kind of decision, take some time to try a *fantasy*. Find a quiet place where you can relax and close your eyes. Then, try to picture two individuals in your mind, arguing the various points on all sides of the question. You may be surprised at the characters your imagination produces—they may not even be people. In any case, pay careful attention to what you visualize in your "mind's eye." What do the fantasy characters look like; how big is each; which argues the loudest and most convincingly? Such a fantasy may tell you a great deal about how you make decisions. Give it a try!

For Further Reading

Kelly, Gary F. *Sexuality Today: The Human Perspective*. Guilford Connecticut: Dushkin Publishing Group, 1992.

Tannen, Deborah. *You Just Don't Understand: Women and Men in Conversation*. New York: William Morrow, 1990.

4 Understanding Same-Sex Attractions and Behaviors

One of the common expectations of our society is that people should be sexually interested only in those of the opposite sex. Again, the facts are different from what the "rule" suggests should be true. There are many who experience sexual interest in someone of their same sex. That interest may be expressed as simple curiosity about the other person's body or through strong feelings of love and attachment that involve sexual desires or actual sexual experience.

Younger boys and girls often play games with one another that lead to undressing or touching each other's sex organs. The old stand-by game of "doctor" is among the most common. As long as one child is not being forced by another to do something he or she does not want to do, and as long as the age difference between the children is not great, such games apparently are generally harmless and represent ways to learn about the body. Sometimes as a part of these games, children of the same sex examine and touch one another.

As children grow older and begin to experience sexual feelings more strongly, there may be some experimentation with sex.

That experimentation may be between youngsters of opposite sexes or of the same sex. It is very common for two boys and two girls to examine each others' bodies, including the sex organs, and to become sexually aroused by doing so. This sometimes leads to masturbating together or other forms of sexual experimentation. For many youth, this is a common occurrence in their development. Such experimentation sometimes occurs in groups of youngsters. Many boys and girls develop a strong interest in and attachment to an adult of either sex. This is a common aspect of development, and such "crushes" generally fade with time.

Some individuals continue to have sexual interest in others of their own sex into adulthood. Many men and women occasionally experience thoughts or fantasies about having sexual contact with others of the same sex. Major studies of sexual behavior tell us that over 20% of men and about 10% of women carry through on these desires at some point in their adult lives and have a same-sex experience to the point of orgasm. Some individuals find that they are generally more aroused sexually by members of their own sex and prefer them as romantic and sexual partners over those of the opposite sex. In fact, up to 10% of adults are predominantly sexually oriented toward members of their own sex.

The Words We Use to Describe Sexual Orientation

The term *heterosexual* is used to describe attractions and activities involving people of the opposite sex. We often make the assumption that people are heterosexual, and so it is not a word that often gets used to label people or the things they do sexually. Attractions or behaviors involving people of the same sex are termed *homosexual*. This word, however, often is used to label people in a very permanent way. The words and labels we use have created a mistaken impression that people are *either-or*: they are either heterosexual in their interests *or* they are homosexual.

Professionals who study human sexuality now know that things are much more complicated than that. Sexual orientation is not just either-or. There are people who may be sexually attracted to, and fall in love with, someone of their own sex. At another time in life, the same individual may become involved with someone of the opposite sex. There are significant numbers of people who have experienced sexual attractions or activities with members of both sexes. This kind of experience is sometimes called *bisexual*. The point is that we cannot neatly place human beings in categories that are clearly labeled as heterosexual, homosexual, or bisexual. Although some individuals may never vary in their sexual interests or attachments, others may become involved with people of different sexes at different times in their lives.

However, it is also true that the majority of human beings have a sexual orientation that predominates, or seems relatively built-in. In common language, people who tend toward heterosexual (opposite-sex) relationships and sexual attractions are called *straight*, whereas those who tend more toward homosexual (same-sex) relationships and attractions are called *gay*. The term gay is sometimes considered to apply more to males, whereas the term *lesbian* is used just with females. Again, however, we have to be careful not to let such labels define people. All people have many more components to their personalities and lives than their sexual orientation. Offensive slang terms about gays and lesbians sometimes are used in everyday conversation as insults or name-calling. We should keep in mind that because we often do not know who is gay, such terms may be very painful even to a friend who has not yet decided how public to be. Though we might never imagine using racial slurs around other people, we seem to have less trouble using bigoted and offensive terms relating to homosexuality.

SAME-SEX ORIENTATION AND OUR SOCIETY

Because we usually make the assumption that children will grow up to be attracted to members of the opposite sex, people who do not fit that mold may find themselves somewhat confused as they are growing up. They may begin to question their own identities as they realize that some of their sexual attractions do not seem to be turning out quite as expected. Some people adjust to being "different" quite easily, whereas others may be afraid of being discovered, and struggle to try and pass as heterosexual.

An individual may become aware of his or her same-sex leanings quite early in life or later. Some homosexual people are aware of their intense feelings a long time before they fully admit the feelings to themselves or others. When a person is concerned or confused about homosexual feelings, it is often helpful to talk with an understanding counselor. It should be realized that individuals who have mostly homosexual feelings cannot usually be persuaded toward having only heterosexual inclinations. However, good counseling can help homosexual and bisexual people to understand and accept their sexuality more completely, and also to choose the kinds of sexual life-styles that suit them best. (See "Finding a Counselor" in Chapter 7.)

Gradually, many people who have a strong same-sex orientation begin to accept it and adjust to it. Because our society still has many negative attitudes about same-sex interests, some homosexual persons decide to be relatively secretive. They may tell close friends or relatives, but not want to be very open with those they cannot fully trust. Having to be secretive about one's sexual orientation has been compared to "being in a closet." Telling others about being gay or lesbian is therefore sometimes called *coming out* of the closet.

Coming out can be a scary process, because one cannot be certain that everyone will accept their same-sex orientation easily. Sometimes, homosexual people find that their parents, other relatives, and friends have difficulty accepting their sexual orientations and may even reject them for a time. More often, others are able to accept them for who they are. It takes good communication to sort out the many issues that may come along when talking about sexual orientation. More about communication in Chapter 7.

These days, many gay and lesbian people have come to accept and live with their same-sex preferences very comfortably. They take pride in their personal lives and their work. They realize that the world is not divided into "us" and "them." They have come to accept that regardless of one's sexual orientation, people can have both positive and negative qualities. Everyone is an individual and deserving of consideration and respect.

What Causes Same-Sex Attraction?

At this point in sex research, we cannot answer the question of how any sexual orientation develops. There is certainly evidence that many people are aware of being attracted to members of the same or the opposite sex quite early in their lives, as children. Some people seem to open up to different sexual experiences during adult life, and find that they either enjoy them or not.

There are several different theories about how we develop our sexual preferences. It was once thought that homosexual orientations were the result of how people were raised or the kinds of sexual experiences they were exposed to when they were growing up. More recent evidence would suggest that family environments or early sexual activities do not shape one's adult sexual orientation very much. In fact, there is an increasing body of research that suggests that some of the tendency toward same-sex or opposite-sex orientations actually may be built in to us by biological factors. Some of these factors may even influence us before we are born.

Among sex researchers, one commonly accepted idea is that same-sex preferences are a normal variation among human beings, less common than heterosexual preference, but not in any way "abnormal." Psychologists generally no longer view same-sex orientation as a problem in itself, although some homosexual persons have difficulty dealing with their orientation because of social pressures. In general, studies show that homosexual people seem to be as psychologically healthy and happy as heterosexual people.

Homophobia and Discrimination

Even in the face of facts about same-sex orientations, there are plenty of negative attitudes about homosexuality. Homosexual people are sometimes called offensive names, or even physically attacked. Many times, such attitudes are simply the result of ignorance, of not having accurate information. Strong negative attitudes or fears about homosexual people have sometimes been called *homophobia*. Such attitudes can lead to discrimination against gays and lesbians and other forms of unfair treatment. In some cities and states in the United States, laws have been passed prohibiting discrimination on the basis of sexual orientation. Many companies and educational institutions have developed programs to combat homophobia and discrimination against homosexual persons and to counteract ignorance.

In recent years, attitudes toward homosexuality have been changing. This has been partly the result of the educational efforts of groups of homosexual people working for gay and lesbian rights. The men and women in these groups have pointed out how unfair laws and social prejudices have caused serious discrimination against homosexual persons. Most states no longer have such laws.

The U.S. military services has excluded people who admitted to being homosexual. However, there is a growing effort within the government to reexamine this policy and eventually change it. Homosexual rights groups insist that one's sexual orientation does not have any bearing on how well a person can do any job or perform in the military.

Myths About Homosexual People

Many myths still exist about people with same-sex orientations. One of those myths is that gay people may be identified by their appearance or mannerisms. In fact, boys who have high-pitched voices, walk with a "girlish" gait, and do not enjoy sports are not necessarily homosexual. Girls who have deeper voices, enjoy sports and outdoor activities, and dress in "boyish" clothes are not necessarily lesbians. Likewise, very strong, "manly" males and dainty, "feminine" females are not necessarily heterosexual. There is apparently no particular relationship between a person's appearance or mannerisms and his or her sexual orientation.

Another myth is that homosexual people "hate" members of the opposite sex. In fact, most gays and lesbians develop friendships—even loving relationships—with those of the opposite sex. Neither are people with same-sex attractions more prone to the seduction of children and teenagers than are heterosexual individuals. Some youngsters—particularly boys—have been frightened by being asked by an adult to participate in some homosexual act. Although this may be upsetting, the older person will seldom push the issue if told, "no, it's just not for me." Studies show that a far greater proportion of sexual approaches to children are made by heterosexuals.

Other false information leads to the belief that all male dancers, hairdressers, and interior decorators are gay, and that all female truck drivers and armed service officers are lesbians. Usually these individuals are simply heterosexuals who have broken through the traditional occupational stereotypes of men and women.

Just because someone is gay or lesbian does not mean that they will be sexually attracted to or aggressive toward every member of their own sex. Homosexual persons generally keep their sexual feelings under control and would not want anyone to feel pressured or embarrassed by their attentions. A homosexual person of your sex is not likely to pressure you into having sex, any more than heterosexual people you know.

Myths are just that: false beliefs that lead people toward misunderstandings and prejudices. Myths often grow from lack of factual information. We owe it to ourselves to make sure that the things we believe and say about same-sex attractions are based on accurate knowledge.

RELATIONSHIPS BETWEEN SAME-SEX PEOPLE

Relationships between people of the same sex usually have been compared to heterosexual relationships, and there is often an assumption made that one person will adopt some sort of "male" role while the other will adopt a "female" role. In fact, relationships between members of the same sex have just as many variations and differences as relationships between those of different sexes. How strong the relationship is, and how long it lasts, will depend on how well the partners get along, how much they have in common, and how committed they are to making the relationship a good one.

When people think about homosexual relationships, they often mistakenly assume that the main connection between the partners is a sexual one. In fact, same-sex couples also enjoy warm, loving companionship, and often maintain close relationships over long periods of time. Some same-sex couples live together for many years, sharing love, sex, household duties, and finances. Such long-term homosexual relationships are much more accepted in our society today than they once were.

Same-sex relationships take many different forms. Sometimes, two persons of the same sex love one another in a romantic sense but choose not to share a sexual relationship. There are also same-sex partners who share a sexual relationship, but do not consider themselves to be gay or lesbian. They simply have found a sexual connection with a particular individual of the same sex, but do not have strong sexual attractions to other members of their sex. And there are homosexual people who share sex, but do not feel any particular romantic love for one another.

Some gay and lesbian couples feel that they should have the right to enter into legally binding relationships such as marriage. There are, for example, some financial and tax advantages for married couples. Although some cities have passed laws that treat same-sex couples in much the same way as heterosexual married couples, actual marriage is still not legally allowed between persons of the same sex. Some religious groups will allow same-sex couples to formalize their commitment to one another in "holy union" ceremonies as public recognition of the value they place on their loving relationship. However, these ceremonies are still not recognized as legally binding. Gay rights groups are not pressing for legalized homosexual marriage so much as they are for laws that will permit same-sex couples to have the same social and economic advantages that married couples are granted.

For a person whose primary sexual and romantic attractions are homosexual, it can be difficult to find others with the same attractions and interests. Again, the social assumption is that everyone is heterosexual, and people who are not may feel frustrated at not being able to identify other homosexual people. In many communities, there are special counseling centers or lesbian and gay groups that can provide support and avenues for interacting with other gay and lesbian individuals. Most cities have a well-developed community of homosexual people who enjoy their lives and offer support to others who are trying to fit into this lifestyle. The organizations listed on pages 255-258 can sometimes be of use in identifying local groups that can help.

Sexual Sharing in Same-Sex Relationships

Partners of the same sex who decide to share sexual experiences have a wide range of sexual activities from which to choose. Just as with heterosexual couples, each partner will have particular preferences, certain turn-ons and turn-offs, when it comes to sex. Contrary to popular opinion, anal sex is not the most popular form of sex between gay males. Lesbians do not usually insert objects into their vaginas as substitutes for a penis. Kissing, hugging, and other touching are common among same-sex couples, as are many other forms of physical sharing. The range of sexual activities is discussed more fully in Chapter 5.

Same-sex partners need to communicate their likes and dislikes to one another, and gradually discover the sexual activities that they enjoy most. Over time, these activities may change as both partners want to explore new things together.

H.I.V. and AIDS Among Homosexual Persons

In the United States, acquired immunodeficiency syndrome, or AIDS, was first identified among the gay male population. The virus that eventually may cause AIDS is H.I.V., or human immunodeficiency virus. H.I.V. is transmitted by direct contact between the body fluids of two people, particularly blood, semen, or vaginal fluids. Unlike many other countries of the world, where AIDS is primarily a disease among heterosexuals, H.I.V. first began being transmitted in the United States between men through sex and between intravenous drug abusers who shared dirty needles contaminated with one another's blood.

Because of the AIDS threat, the gay and lesbian community responded quickly with educational efforts, warning same-sex partners about the risks of infection and how to avoid them. The rate of infection in these groups began to decrease right away. It is important to emphasize now that *H.I.V. infection and AIDS are NOT just diseases of the homosexual population anymore*. Infection with H.I.V. has instead reached alarming rates among heterosexual people, particularly women and teenagers. Chapter 8 will provide you with the facts about H.I.V. and AIDS. Be sure to read it!

This is not to say that gay and lesbian couples need not be cautious. In any sort of sexual encounter, it is crucial to consider the risks of being infected by H.I.V. The safest choice to make would be to forgo sex altogether until you can be absolutely certain that your partner does not carry the virus. For couples who do decide to have sex, it will be important to choose sexual activities in which the risk of sharing bodily fluids is at a minimum, and to use protections such as condoms that can provide barriers against such fluids. Nobody can afford to have sex these days without taking all the precautions possible to protect themselves from H.I.V. infection.

Specific suggestions for protecting yourself from H.I.V. and AIDS are given in Chapter 8.

IF YOU THINK YOU MIGHT BE GAY OR LESBIAN

When you are growing and developing as a sexual person, it is not easy to begin realizing that you may somehow be different from what you, your parents, or your society expected of you. Because social expectations still tend to make the assumption that everyone is heterosexual, you gradually will have to come to grips with what your sexuality means for you and your life. If you think you might have some same-sex attractions and interests, here are some suggestions to keep in mind:

1. Being attracted sexually to members of your own sex is not something that you had any control over. It is not something you chose. As stated earlier in this chapter, even the experts really do not know how sexual orientation develops.

2. Sexual orientation is not necessarily either-or. To have some same-sex attractions is very common. You will have to sort out how strong the attractions are and how much you want to act on them. You may find attractions to members of the opposite sex too. Again, it will be up to you to find the balance in these attractions that seems to suit your life.

3. What kinds of relationships you have, and what sorts of sexual experiences you become involved in, always will be a matter of choice. You can have control over these aspects of your life. However, it is important to keep in mind that you eventually will have to achieve some sense of inner peace between your inner needs and the life choices you make. It will be important not to waste too much of your energy pretending to be someone you're not. You will need to be honest with and accepting of yourself, and with those who are closest to you. Again, the sexual choices you make are always up to you. But inside, it will be important for you to be comfortable with them.

4. How open you are with your homosexual feelings will be up to you. Some individuals decide that they want to be completely open, and if others cannot accept them for who they are that is okay. Others choose to be more careful about whom they let know. The bottom line is that your sexual orientation is a private matter. How many others you let know about your sexuality is completely up to you.

5. If you feel some confusion and turmoil about your sexual attractions, it would be a good idea to find a trusted person with whom to talk over your feelings. It is a good idea to choose someone whom you know can be comfortable with the issue of homosexuality, and who will not have a personal stake in trying to persuade you in some particular direction. For more ideas on choosing a good person with whom to talk, consult the section in this book called "Finding a Counselor" on pages 142–145.

6. Beginning to admit to yourself and accept homosexual feelings does not have to be a tragedy. It certainly does not have to mean that your life is over. Instead, it can represent a beginning: an opportunity to get to know yourself better and to create for yourself a future that will involve self-acceptance, self-respect, and an honest sense of who you are and what you have to offer. Don't ever let people around you fool you into thinking that this part of your personality is something you must be ashamed of. That is not the case.

WHAT DO YOU THINK?

1. Here is a list of some current issues in our society. What are your opinions on these issues?
   (a) Should homosexual couples be allowed to marry?
   (b) Should gay and lesbian couples be allowed to adopt and raise children?
   (c) Should homosexual people be allowed to serve in the military?

2. Try to project yourself into the following situations and think carefully about what you would think and do. How do your imagined actions reflect your feelings and values?

    (a) One afternoon you are talking alone with your best friend of your same sex. Your friend confides to you that she or he has homosexual feelings.

    (b) You are away at college (or summer camp, or working in a city) and your roommate tells you after two weeks that you probably should know that he or she is gay/lesbian.

    (c) One of your teachers of your same sex has become a good friend. One afternoon while talking together casually, she/he gently puts a hand on your shoulder and leaves it there for several seconds.

    (d) Go back to situations (a) and (c) and try to consider what your reactions would be if the other person was of the opposite sex.

For Further Reading

Eichberg, R. *Coming Out: An Act of Love*. New York: Penguin Books, 1990.

Fairchild, B. and N. Hayward. *Now That You Know: What Every Parent Should Know About Homosexuality*. San Diego, California: Harcourt Brace Jovanovich, 1989.

Fricke, Aaron. *Reflections of a Rock Lobster: A Story About Growing Up Gay*. Boston: Alyson Publications, 1981.

Garden, Nancy. *Annie on My Mind* (a fictional story of love between two adolescent girls). New York: Farrar, Straus, and Giroux, 1982.

Geller, T. *Bisexuality: A Reader and Sourcebook*. Ojai, California: Times Change Press, 1990.

McNaught, Brian. *A Disturbed Peace: Selected Writings of an Irish Catholic Homosexual*. Washington, D.C: Dignity Inc., 1981.

— — *On Being Gay: Thoughts on Family, Faith, and Love*. New York: St. Martin's Press, 1988.

5 Sharing Our Sexual Feelings and Behaviors

Because our sexuality is a part of our total personality, we bring that sexuality with us to every contact we have with another human being. In some of those contacts, we find ourselves more in touch with our actual sexual feelings and find ourselves sexually aroused, or "turned-on" by the other person. The other person may be experiencing the same kind of interest, and then some decisions may be made about how much sharing of sexual feelings you both want to have.

LEVELS OF SHARING

Before exploring the decision-making process, it will be important to explore the different levels of sexual sharing. We shall begin with the more superficial levels and move to the deeper levels, involving more closeness and sense of personal intimacy. It is usually safe to assume that deeper levels of sharing bring with them more risks and responsibilities to be considered carefully and thoughtfully.

An important part of early sexual sharing with another is *talking together*. This usually continues into deeper levels of sharing as well. Often, open communication of thoughts and feelings leads to the desire for more intimacy. Yet, such communication can be scary too. It takes courage to let another person in on what we are feeling and thinking. There is much more on communication about sex in Chapter 7.

After talking together, the decision might be reached that there is no point in moving to deeper levels of sexual sharing. Often, however, two people move on to some form of *body contact*. It is usually very exciting and exhilarating to get physically closer to someone whom you care about and feel sexually attracted to. For many couples, this contact begins with kissing and hugging. Sometimes during kissing, one partner may move his or her tongue into the other's mouth, often called "French kissing." Because H.I.V., the virus that causes AIDS, has been found in saliva, experts are urging caution about the sharing of saliva during kissing. However, the risk of getting H.I.V. through kissing is considered to be very low. All of us have our own preferences about how we like to be kissed and where we most enjoy being touched. As two people get to know each other, talking and other signals that develop help to convey those preferences to one another.

Two people who enjoy physical closeness eventually may move toward touching many parts of each other's bodies, including the sex organs. The more touching the two people do, the more apt they are to become intensely aroused sexually. Even with very little physical contact—or just thinking about a person he finds attractive—a boy may experience sexual excitement and erection of his penis. Girls may also experience sensations of increased tension and sexual arousal of their bodies when they are physically close to someone they find attractive or are thinking about that person.

It should be kept in mind that some people may not want certain parts of their body touched, and they certainly have the right to avoid such contact. As sexual sharing deepens, it is up to both partners to be sensitive to the messages from one another that indicate pleasure or displeasure. Some couples eventually progress to stimulating one another's sex organs. This is done not only with the hands, but sometimes with the mouth. It may also refer to touching a girl's breasts. Sometimes, the touching is done through the clothing. Other times, one partner may reach inside the other's clothing or both may decide to remove their clothing. Of course, being in the nude with another person may be somewhat awkward and uncomfortable at first, but it may also be intensely pleasurable and highly sexually exciting. This represents a very deep level of sexual sharing, which may carry with it strong emotions and the need for responsible decision-making.

An even deeper level of sharing comes with sexual activity in which one or both of the partners may reach orgasm. Most everyone feels that such activity is an important step in the process of sexual sharing. Yet many couples decide to postpone it for a variety of reasons, and they confine their pleasurable sharing to mutual touching without orgasm or lighter levels of sharing. It should be remembered, however, that sexual feelings are powerful, and once we become sexually aroused, it may be much more difficult to spend much time thinking through decisions. For that reason, it is probably wise to clarify our values and our ideas about responsibility before we place ourselves in a situation that produces intense sexual excitement.

Perhaps the level of sexual sharing that is deepest of all is the one that involves loving feelings for the other person. This leads to the gentle, warm sharing of the deepest parts of ourselves. That kind of sharing may be a part of sexual activity and the quiet being together following orgasm, but not necessarily. It may also be a part of any other level of sexual sharing, regardless of how much body contact is involved. While I was writing this chapter, a friend said to me, "Let's not give young people the idea that sex is just intercourse. My wife and I love to give each other massages, and that is a really great sexual experience!" I truly hope that this whole book will help to convey that very message: sex *is* far more than intercourse or any other form of sexual activity leading to orgasm.

Foundations of Sexual Activity

It can be difficult to find realistic information about what actually happens in sex, and few people readily discuss their own sexual experiences. Consequently, many young people find that sex is a rather mysterious thing. Even when it is described in books or portrayed in photographs or movies, the facts may be considerably distorted. The media tend to depict sexual activity as simple and always supremely pleasurable. In actuality, sexual activity that yields the maximum pleasure to both partners may take a considerable amount of learning, communication, and time, and may have nothing to do with the capacity of the individuals to "perform" sexually. Instead, it may depend more on the quality of the personal relationship between the people involved.

Because of the distorted view of sex that many people develop, or for other reasons, their first sexual experiences may be quite disappointing. Or, first experiences might be quite wonderful and exciting, and later experiences may be disappointing because they lack the same quality of discovery. Both kinds of disappointment may lead to discouragement and real sexual problems. So it makes sense to learn as much about the various forms of sexual activity as possible before deciding whether or not to engage in them.

Perhaps one of the most important foundations for enjoyable and meaningful sex is that *both partners really want it to happen.* They really want it to happen not because they are rushed into it, but because they have thought through their decisions carefully and shared their thoughts, feelings, and values with one another. In other words, neither partner is being persuaded into any sexual activity by reasons such as fear of losing the other person, wanting to prove that one is now grown up, doing it because one's friends are, or one's selfish manipulations to "get it" from the other.

Another necessary foundation for meaningful sex is an atmosphere of relaxation, externally and internally. The external setting must be one that enables both partners to feel happy, comfortable, and good about themselves. A physically uncomfortable place, such as a cramped car seat, or an atmosphere that necessitates hurrying, such as the fear of getting caught, probably will not produce a fully pleasurable experience. Likewise, both partners should be as free from internal worries and conflicts as possible. If either person feels frightened, guilty, or as if he or she is doing something wrong, then perhaps more time should be given to the decision of whether or not to have sex. It is also important to note that body hygiene is necessary for many people to enjoy sex (fresh breath, no perspiration odor, clean sex organs).

Part of the mystery that some young people face about sex is not knowing what happens during sexual activity. Actually, it is difficult to explain in a general way, because each individual must learn at some point what sex is all about for himself or herself. I shall try, however, to describe what may happen as clearly as possible. To understand this section fully, be certain that you have read about male and female anatomy in Chapter 2 and about the body's stages of sexual response in Chapter 3.

Remembering and Reducing the Risks of Sex

Because of H.I.V. infection, AIDS, and the other sexually transmitted diseases discussed more fully in Chapter 8, it is important to stop and think about the risks before you proceed with any sexual sharing on the physical level. The germs that cause infection, including H.I.V.—the virus that can lead to AIDS—are carried by the body fluids that mingle during sexual activity. These fluids include semen, the clear fluid that may seep out of the penis before ejaculation, and fluids within the vagina. H.I.V. also may be found in the rectum and anal area of an infected individual.

The first step to sexual sharing must always be an honest, realistic consideration of the risks you are facing. This chapter, along with Chapter 8, will present you with many issues to weigh carefully before you take sexual risks with your emotions or your physical health. Although there are ways of making sexual sharing safer, there is always some degree of risk. One way to avoid the risks is by abstinence—avoiding the kind of intense sexual sharing that might have dangerous consequences. Another way to at least reduce the risks is to make certain that you do not come into contact with fluids or wet places of the other person. To prevent fluid contact, rubber condoms may be worn by males, and females will soon have available a pouch-like "female condom" that may be inserted into the vagina prior to sexual contact. Chapter 8 (pages 158–160) offers more details on how you may be able to reduce the risks of sexual sharing.

FORMS OF PHYSICAL SEXUAL SHARING

This section of the chapter describes the various ways in which people participate in physical sexual sharing. You probably will have heard many different slang terms used to describe these activities.

Foreplay

Preceding a period of heightened sexual activity, the couple usually spends some time deepening their levels of sexual sharing. Typically, that begins with kissing, caressing, and petting. These activities usually increase sexual excitement in both partners. You will remember that sexual excitement is characterized by erection of the penis in males and secretion of fluid along the inner walls of the vagina in females. The period before attempting orgasm is often referred to as "foreplay" and may last only a few minutes or for a much longer time. During that time, the degree of sexual arousal in both partners may increase and decrease several times.

Mutual Masturbation

Part of the period of foreplay usually includes touching of the partner's sexual organs, and such touching may also lead to orgasm by means of mutual masturbation (see Chapter 3). Although this way of reaching orgasm is most common among young people who are experimenting with sex, or among those who wish to avoid other forms of sexual activity for some reason, some couples continue to enjoy mutual masturbation to orgasm throughout an extended relationship. It may be used as a way of varying their sexual activity.

Sexual Intercourse

A common form of sexual activity for heterosexual couples is sexual intercourse, which refers to the insertion of a man's penis into a woman's vagina. This insertion may take a little time and some gentle effort, depending on the size of the vagina and the amount of lubrication. If the woman has not experienced intercourse before and the hymen is still present, the penis may rupture the hymen, and the woman *may* experience some discomfort and a small amount of bleeding (see page 33).

After the penis is comfortably inside the vagina, the two partners move rhythmically in ways that give both pleasant sensations. Usually, both partners move their pelvises in a way that moves the penis in and out of the vagina. These pelvic movements may be varied from slow and gentle rhythms to rapid, vigorous thrusting. Which partner controls the movements and the rate depends partly on the position of the two people. Sexual intercourse may take place in a great variety of positions. Couples often enjoy experimenting to find the positions that are most comfortable and enjoyable for them. One of the myths that we often hear wild stories about is that the vagina sometimes contracts so the penis becomes caught inside, and the two people are unable to separate. This is completely untrue and does not occur. Because male dogs have a different penis structure than humans, they do become temporarily "caught" during mating, but this is an important part of successful breeding in dogs.

During intercourse, the bodies of both the male and female usually go through all of the expected stages of sexual response.

Males nearly always reach orgasm during intercourse, and since they then usually lose their erections, intercourse is finished for them until after the refractory period has ended. Some females do not reach orgasm each time they have intercourse. For some women, this is a real concern whereas for others it apparently does not matter. Some women also have more than one orgasm during intercourse. Women may want to continue intercourse after reaching orgasm because they have no refractory period and do not have to maintain an erection. This is not to say, however, that women should not play a part in deciding when intercourse should continue or when it should cease. It should be noted that most people at one time or another experience some problems in having sexual intercourse. Some typical problems are discussed in Chapters 7 and 10.

Oral Sex

Oral sexual contact means using the mouth or tongue to touch or stimulate another person's sex organs. It can involve taking the male penis into the mouth; sometimes called *fellatio*, or using the tongue to stimulate the female clitoris or vagina, sometimes called *cunnilingus*. Although oral stimulation may be used as a prelude to other sexual activity leading to orgasm, it is also a common way of achieving orgasm for both males and females.

It would appear from the studies of sex researchers that a majority of people find oral sexual contact to be pleasurable and acceptable. Others find the idea of oral sex disgusting or immoral. Like so many other aspects of sexual behavior, this is often an area that partners must discuss with one another amd come to some mutual decisions about. One partner should not be coerced into any sexual activity against his or her will. Basic rules of cleanliness and hygiene should be observed for oral sex, as well as the consideration of serious concerns about the possible transmission of H.I.V. in this manner. If an individual carries the virus, there may be some possibility of it being transmitted through oral sexual contact. See the discussion about AIDS in Chapter 8.

Anal Sex

Anal sex refers to the insertion of the male penis into the anus of his partner. It is a form of sexual behavior that may sometimes be shared by male partners and by heterosexual couples. As with oral sex, some people find anal sex to be immoral and disgusting. It is a sexual practice that has been implicated in the transmission of H.I.V. from infected men to their partners. The risk may be particularly high because of possible tissue damage in the rectum from anal intercourse. Again, be certain to read the discussion about H.I.V. and AIDS in Chapter 8. For couples choosing to share anal sex, wearing a condom is always advisable. Unlike the vagina, the anus does not have its own source of lubrication, thus great gentleness and care must be taken, and a lubricating substance is often necessary for insertion. Because bacteria live in the rectum, the penis should not be inserted in the vagina or mouth following anal insertion, without being washed first.

After Sex

The length of time spent in sexual activity leading to orgasm varies with different couples and different situations. It is obvious that one of the common time-determining factors is the length of time it takes to reach orgasm. In any case, such activity may last less than a minute or for much longer periods of time, even up to an hour or more. Again, both partners should cooperate in finding the length of time that is best for each of them, and that may vary at different times.

Most couples find that the togetherness before and after orgasm is very important for the expression of warm, loving feelings toward one another. Not only may sexual activity help an individual feel that his or her body is desirable and cared for, it may also lead to a strengthening of the total relationship. It is not, however, a substitute for the real work of building a meaningful relationship, nor is it an adequate way of solving the real problems that arise when two people are trying to be important to each other.

SEX AND YOUR VALUES

Until recent years, one of the predominant values of American society was that a couple should not engage in sexual activity before, or outside of, marriage. Many people did not abide by that value, however, and some of them felt very guilty about not doing so. There are still many religious groups and individuals who feel that sexual activity outside of marriage is morally wrong. There are others who believe that marriage and religious convictions are not the issues, but that sex outside of a responsible, committed relationship in which there is love and caring, is ultimately unrewarding.

There has been another attitude about sex in our society for many years. It is also present in many other cultures. This is the view that young men are more likely to have casual sexual experiences than are young women. In a variety of ways—through the media, their peers, and sometimes their parents—boys are led to believe that casual sex is not only all right for them, but that there is something wrong with them if they don't have it. Yet, the same is not true for girls. Instead, messages are conveyed to them that "nice" girls not only do not have casual sex, but that they shouldn't have any desire for it. This whole confusing, unfair set of values is called the *double standard*. There are, of course, many other double standards for males and females, many of them as equally absurd. Take, for example, the idea that it is all right for girls to hug and kiss each other as ways of showing friendliness and affection, but that is not all right for boys.

Attitudes and values about sex have gone through many shifts within recent years. That is not to say that many people now do not feel that sexual activity before marriage is wrong. They do. However, others believe that marriage in itself should not be the "justification" for sex. Instead, these people believe it is the quality of the relationship, the levels of risk for sex, and the maturity of the two people in it that should determine whether sexual activity is the "right" step.

Like most other decisions about sex, whether or not to engage in sexual activity, either before marriage or outside of a
committed relationship, will have to be *your* decision. Although
on the surface it may seem to be a simple decision, there may be
many issues that deserve careful consideration. For example, it
will probably be necessary for you to weigh into your decision the
moral values of your parents, religious teachings, community,
peers, and of your potential sex partner. It will be crucial to think
carefully about possible risks of catching H.I.V. As I stated earlier,
although sex carries with it extreme pleasure and joy, it also has
the potential for hurting ourselves and others. I have talked with
many young people who have been emotionally hurt to some
degree by sex, usually because they have not had adequate opportunities to figure out what they want before becoming deeply
involved with sex. I have talked with people who wish more than
anything they could take back the sexual decision that led to
pregnancy or H.I.V. infection. I have also talked with many people
who have found sex to be a happy bond in their relationships. In
the following section, I hope you will consider the possible consequences—positive and negative—of embarking on sexual
experiences.

Deciding About Sex

Making the decision about whether or not to have sex used to
be simpler when society's values were more clear-cut. As one of my
students once said, "Even if you did it, at least you didn't have to
worry about whether you were right or wrong. You knew you were
wrong!" It would be easier if I could just list all the right reasons
and all the wrong reasons for you, but that cannot be done. In fact, I
can only describe what some of the *possible* consequences could
be. Think about each of them and how each might fit for your life.

First, let's take a look at some possible negative
consequences:

1. *Unwanted pregnancy*

    This is always a possibility any time intercourse takes place. Birth control methods (see Chapter 9) reduce the risks of pregnancy, but they cannot eliminate them completely. If an unwanted pregnancy occurs, very difficult decisions must be faced concerning alternative routes of action: abortion, adoption, marriage, or single parenthood. The problem of an unwanted pregnancy may occur within marriage as well as before.

2. *Possibility of disease*

    The incidence of sexually transmitted disease, STD, is on the rise. These infections are discussed in more detail in Chapter 8. If a sexual partner is chosen who has shared sex with someone else, there may be a risk that he or she has a sexually transmitted disease. Although treatment is available for most STDs, there is no known cure for H.I.V. disease or AIDS. This makes it crucial to be extremely cautious about sexual partners whose possible earlier sexual encounters are not known, or who may be at risk of carrying the virus. See the discussion of H.I.V. and AIDS in Chapter 8.

3. *Unexpected emotional involvement*

    Even casual sexual activity often produces intense emotional reactions, even if those reactions are not wanted. Intimate physical contact sometimes generates strong emotional attachments that may be difficult for both partners to cope with. For some young people, sexual activity is mistakenly interpreted as a sign of long-lasting commitment to the relationship. This is simply another reason why good communication between people is so essential *before* sex takes place.

4. *Guilt and regret*

    Let's face it: plenty of people still feel guilty and regretful about sexual experiences, especially if they are violating moral codes of their parents or their religion. Guilt doesn't help people to feel good about themselves and may eventually be quite destructive. Each individual must carefully consider the potential of sex producing guilt in his or her life, and attempt to pursue relationships which will not be regretted later.

5. *Feeling "conned" or used*

   Sexual activity that is positive and healthy takes place as a matter of choice in an atmosphere of mutual honesty and trust. It is unfortunate that some people—both males and females—view the persuasion of another person into sex as some sort of conquest, or as a way to hold on to the other person. Not only are these poor reasons for sexual activity, but it is almost inevitable that the other partner will eventually feel as if he or she has been "conned" and used.

   Now, we may consider some of the possible positive consequences of sexual activity. It should be emphasized that positive consequences are generally possible only in the context of a loving, committed relationship between the two people involved.

   You should also keep in mind that sexual activity is *only one of the ways in which the following may be achieved:*

1. *Learning the pleasure of sexual sharing*

   In the context of a healthy, loving relationship, sexual activity can often provide new heights of physical and emotional pleasure.

2. *Feeling good about your body*

   When we get pleasure from our bodies while giving another person pleasure, we often feel more positively about what our bodies have to offer. Additionally, when we feel that our body is attractive and sexually desirable to another, we generally feel good about it.

3. *Deepening the sense of intimacy and caring*

   In a relationship that involves real intimacy and caring, sexual activity can be an expression of these feelings, and can deepen them. If the relationship is the one of giving and getting it should be, then sexual activity can symbolize this relationship, and both partners may feel more closely involved than ever before.

4. *Learning about sexual functioning*

Many individuals learn a great deal about their body's sexual responsiveness during shared sexual activity. Some girls and women do not experience orgasm until they have had sexual experience with another person. There are studies that show that premarital intercourse can lead to more rapid sexual adjustment after marriage, though not necessarily a better adjustment. Some people in committed relationships report that they are glad of having had previous sexual experience, while others regret such experience and feel that it was not helpful to them.

5. *Learning about sexual responsibility*

Some young people report that previous sexual experience helped them to learn about the responsibilities they must take in deeper, more committed relationships. Often, they report that they have learned by making some mistakes with sex. Because most people know how "mistakes" with sex may so strongly affect lives, they hope that others will make as few mistakes as possible. Yet, maybe the most important suggestions I can give you are to try to prevent mistakes by thinking carefully about your decisions and to learn whatever you can from your own mistakes or those of others.

Not Having Sex

The facts are that many young people—even those involved in long-term relationships—are not having sex. We live in pressured times sexually, and sometimes it is difficult to keep in mind that *it is okay not to have sex.* Plenty of young people who take the time to think through their decisions and to discuss sex with their partners decide that sexual activity will have to be postponed until later. Some couples decide to give one another sexual pleasure through mutual masturbation, whereas others limit themselves to less intense levels of sharing such as kissing and hugging.

It should also be noted that neither marriage nor any other form of committed relationship insures a great sexual relationship. Sexual problems and frustrations are commonly brought to marriage counselors and sex therapists. In a relationship where the two people are truly committed to one another and want to improve their sexual sharing, sex may usually be improved and made to be much less of problem.

It is not a simple matter to make decisions about sex. Often, there is downright confusion and misunderstanding. Hopefully, the exercises at the end of this chapter will help you to think through your values on these issues.

Are You Ready?

If you come to a point in your life when you are interested in sharing sex with another person, you will want to consider the following areas. They are things that should be thought about and that you might want to discuss with your potential partner:

1. What do you expect from your partner in the way of love and caring, and what does your partner expect of you? Check any of the following that apply to the directions your relationship seems to be taking:

   _____ We love each other.

   _____ We're trying to understand what love means to us.

   _____ We probably won't ever be married, but we are working on a committed relationship.

   _____ We expect to be married when that is possible.

   _____ I sometimes am not certain if he/she cares about me as much as I care back.

   _____ I feel pressured to have sex, even though I'm not sure I'm ready.

   _____ We've already done a lot of fooling around, but we are postponing more serious sex until we are more ready.

_____ Because one of us has shared sex with another partner, we need to consider how much risk there is of transmitting H.I.V. or other infections.

_____ We've already had some intense sex together, but we're not sure we want to again right away.

_____ We have intercourse regularly, and plan to continue to do so.

_____ We do not plan to have intercourse until after we're married.

_____ I sometimes don't think that he/she enjoys sexual contact as much as I do.

_____ I sometimes worry about possible pregnancy.

2. The following is a list of what most professionals consider to be poor reasons in themselves for having sex with another person. Think carefully about whether or not any of them *could be* your reasons or your partner's:

    (a) To improve the relationship
    (b) To prove that you are a responsible adult
    (c) To feel independent from parents
    (d) To rebel against traditional values
    (e) To show that you really love the other person
    (f) To go along with what others seem to be doing
    (g) To prove that you're good at sex
    (h) To prevent your partner from leaving you
    (i) To prove you are a "real" man or woman

3. Are you ready to accept consequences such as an unwanted pregnancy? Are you able to discuss birth control with your partner? What form of birth control have you decided to use? How effective is it (see Chapter 9)?

4. If you decide to share sexual activity, how much deceit will be involved? Are you going to have to lie about where you are going, and if so—how do you feel about lying?

5. Have you weighed into the decision the moral values of your parents? your religion? your school and community? your peers? your partner? What about H.I.V. and AIDS?

6. Make a list—in writing—of what your goals would be in having sex with someone. Have your partner make such a list too. When both lists are finished, get together, compare them, and talk about what you have learned.
7. Consider the following spectrum of sexual values. Try to locate on each line whether you fall at one extreme or the other. Do you consider yourself somewhere in between:

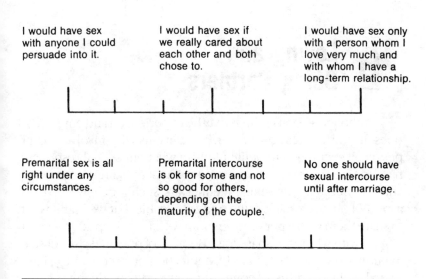

I would have sex with anyone I could persuade into it.

I would have sex if we really cared about each other and both chose to.

I would have sex only with a person whom I love very much and with whom I have a long-term relationship.

Premarital sex is all right under any circumstances.

Premarital intercourse is ok for some and not so good for others, depending on the maturity of the couple.

No one should have sexual intercourse until after marriage.

For Further Reading

Fiedler, Jean and Hal Fiedler. *Be Smart About Sex*. Hillside, New Jersey: Enslow Publishers, 1990.

Starkman, Neal. *Your Decision*. Seattle, Washington: Comprehensive Health Education Foundation, 1988.

6 Loving and Being Partners

Although sexual feelings may be experienced and enjoyed by oneself, full expression of our sexuality usually involves other people. It seems that to delight fully in what our sexual responses have to offer, there needs to be a sharing of those responses with another. Because our sexual feelings are such a deeply personal aspect of our selves, it is quite understandable that we might want to share them with a person for whom we have a deep affection—a person with whom we share love. Because of potential risks of sex, including the possibility of H.I.V. infection, it is crucial to share sexual feelings with someone we know and trust deeply.

In this chapter, we will take a look at love, intimacy, and partnerships, and at how they relate to our lives as sexual people. This is a tall order, for there are a number of fine books on these subjects, and for centuries authors and poets have dealt with the myriad intricacies and complexities of love. It is a confusing subject, and most of us experience some very real confusion and hurt as we try to deal with loving feelings at various times in our lives. I have talked with hundreds of people—young, old, and in between—who were attempting to understand loving relationships in their lives. Often, the part that sex plays in those relationships is a major concern.

WHAT IS LOVE?

It seems that the word "love" has become a catchall term in our language. The Eskimos have fifteen different words to describe different types of the substance we call simply *snow*. Surely we could use that many different words to do justice to the many aspects of love that we experience. I talk of loving my parents and my brother; I love my wife and my dog; I often say that I love a certain book, or a movie, or a piece of music. We hear about loving God and of loving humankind. Many people use the term "making love" to refer to having sexual intercourse. Surely these forms of love differ in many respects.

It has been suggested that love is an *art*. In other words, it is not enough just to sit back and wait to get lucky and "fall in love." Instead, we must spend time *learning* what love is and what it means to our lives. It is essential that we put real *effort* into loving others; love is something that must be worked at! To be successful with love, we must actively practice it as an art worthy of our careful attention.

We live in a society where love and sex are important topics. That is easy to notice when we examine the themes of books, videos, movies, music, magazine stories, television shows, and even advertising. Love is everywhere! It is also portrayed much of the time in very unrealistic ways; it is often made to seem simple and uncomplicated—once the love conflict in the story line is resolved, the couple lives happily ever after without having to *work* at love again. As most of us can testify, love is usually entered into with great hopes and expectations and promises, yet hardly any human venture ends in failure as often as does love.

Falling in Love and Being in Love

Think for a moment about all of the people you have seen in the past week, or in your lifetime. How many of them could you say you know? How many could be called "friend"? Probably not very many of them. It is part of the human condition that most of us are strangers to one another. We are separate; we are isolated. In some ways, we are alone. Some of us feel that separateness more acutely than others, but for most of us there is an inner longing to be closer to others. That longing may be shown through the desire to "belong" or "fit in" with a group of people our own age. It may be seen in the need to play a sport that has a team spirit. And with its greatest intensity, the longing may be felt at times as a deep need to become emotionally and physically closer to a particular person.

Whenever I have an encounter with another human being that involves the lowering of our barriers—allowing us to see each other more honestly and openly without the usual masks and hidden emotions—I feel marvelously happy and exhilarated. I am not as separate; my longing for closeness is, for a time, quieted. This is part of the process of "falling in love"—a relatively sudden and intense feeling of intimacy and closeness. It feels good, and sometimes the sexual attraction or sharing of sexual feelings that may become a part of such an encounter make it all feel even better. Sometimes, the excitement of falling in love is called *infatuation*.

However, we never "fall" forever. The falling in love process is not a lasting one. For awhile, the two people continue to break through more and more barriers, getting closer and closer. But eventually the process becomes less exciting and interesting. Even sexual involvement gradually loses some of its luster. If the individuals have not moved more toward a lasting state of "being in love," their mutual boredom and disappointment will end the falling process, and there will be little left to keep them together.

So, now, what is this "being in love" all about? Everyone must discover what this real loving is going to be for their own lives. I am working on it in my life and will be for a long time to come. Yet, by talking about love with a wide variety of people—alone and in couples—I have come to believe that there are certain elements that seem to be common to any relationship where people are *working* at being in love.

Qualities of Being in Love

1. *Choice*

   We consciously choose what people we can let ourselves be fully close to, and we choose how much of ourselves we feel able to show to any other person. But the choice must be mutual if it is to be love. All individuals involved in the loving relationship must choose one another.

2. *Giving*

   To love, we must give to another. This does not mean giving up or sacrificing, nor does it just mean giving objects or money. Instead, there is a mutual giving of qualities of one's life: experiences, feelings, humor, sadness, and all things that are a part of us. Giving brings us joy and it enriches us; it helps bring us closer.

3. *Closeness*

   People in love strive for more honest knowledge of each other—knowledge of their past experiences, of ideas and values, of feelings and hopes, of weaknesses and defects and disappointments, of what their bodies have to offer. To reach continuously new depths of intimacy requires *time, privacy,* and *trust*.

4. *Trust*

   We come to trust another as we gradually risk revealing our inner thoughts and feelings to that other person. In love, if the other person treats what we reveal with care, gentleness, and respect, we learn to feel a sense of trust. Mutual trust seems to be essential to being in love.

5. *Caring*

   Being in love also means being actively concerned for the person whom we love: concerned for that individual's feelings and needs. People who love care about seeing each other grow and be happy and fulfilled.

6. *Responsibility*

    When we choose to be close to another individual and care about him or her, then we have accepted a degree of responsibility to respond to that other person's needs. I do not mean that this is in any way a duty. Instead it is a *willingness* to be responsive to another human being. The other side of responsibility is letting our needs be known to those who love us, so that they can then respond.

7. *Respect*

    This is a quality that is often misunderstood. When I respect others, it does not mean that I do what they want because I am afraid of them. It means that I see them as the unique individuals they are. It means that I will want to see the other person emerge as he or she is, as fully as possible.

8. *Delight*

    Loving involves mutual delight as we care for one another and share and watch one another emerge. When we allow another person to grow or give him or her pleasure, then we delight in ourselves and in each other.

9. *Self-awareness*

    It seems that the more we know about ourselves, the more we can understand what is happening between us and others. Being in love necessitates a continuing struggle to keep in touch with what is happening inside ourselves. In that way, what we give to one another is clearer and more meaningful.

Those are at least some of the qualities people in love find to be important if the relationship is to be a lasting one. There are many other words that could be used, and you may have other qualities you would want to add to the list. Feel free to do so. You may also feel that I am pointing toward some sort of perfection that is not very plausible for most people. Maybe, but I have seen a great many people make remarkable progress in establishing good loving relationships. Of course, we all have to struggle with these qualities, but I believe that struggle is part of what love is all about.

Perhaps the most important point of all is that to achieve any measure of success with these qualities, *work* is required. By work I mean being consciously aware of what you are trying to accomplish, concentrating on your goals, and having as much patience as you can muster because it won't be quick or easy. I also mean working at these qualities even when it is a little difficult, even though you may not be quite "in the mood."

Over the years in my own life I have realized that I just cannot sit back and wait for "love" to fall in my lap. I am going to have to try consciously to make my relationships with other persons good for us—to make them loving. And I am also realizing that it is very worth the effort.

Whom Do We Love?

It seems, then, that loving another person involves the *total relationship* you share with that person, along with the relationships you share with others. There are also different types of love, each based on the type of person or object that is being loved. Let us consider briefly six kinds of love that seem to be a part of human experience:

1. *Love for humankind*
   This is the kind of love for others we feel as we realize that all of us have a great deal in common. When we really feel our connection and equality with our fellow humans, we can begin to care about them.
2. *Love of God*
   In most religions, this goes hand-in-hand with loving our fellow humans. It is often emphasized in religions that love of God is shown by a feeling of oneness with a divine being which is expressed in the actions the person takes.
3. *Love for someone we can help*
   It is this sort of love that a mother and father feel for their child or that you might feel for a younger brother or sister.

4. *Love of parents*

   This is an example of the kind of love we feel toward someone who has protected us and taken care of us when we needed help.

5. *Love for oneself*

   This is often misunderstood and confused with conceit. It does not refer to the sort of thing I once saw in a student of mine. He was always saying, "I am great!" Instead, it means having self-respect and being able to trust in your own actions; it means caring about what happens to you as well as others around you. Many psychologists believe that before you can be a truly complete person and before you can really work at loving others, you must first care for yourself.

6. *Love with sexual longing*

   This is the kind of love that involves the desire to share sexually with another person—to feel the closeness and excitement a sexual union can achieve. It is more than the pleasure of bodies physically being together, but includes all of the emotional aspects of people deepening their levels of communication and mutual delight.

Where Does Sex Fit?

Now we need to take a look at how sex fits—or doesn't fit—into this picture. One of the perennial questions has been: Can sex have real meaning without love? In fact, there are a great many ways in which people enjoy the excitement of their own sexual feelings and the sharing of those feelings with others without many aspects of love being present at all.

For example, almost all boys and the majority of girls begin to get in touch with their sexual feelings and the enjoyment they can yield through masturbation. This refers to stimulating the sexual organs with the hands or in some other way to produce sexual stimulation and the pleasure of sexual climax or orgasm (also see Chapter 3). Masturbation, along with the fantasies that may accompany it in the mind, may be intensely pleasurable and exciting ways of expressing our sexuality, and yet love has little to do with it.

Likewise, some people have enjoyed casual sexual encounters with others. Without any emotional involvement or loving feelings expected, some agree to share sex with one another and enjoy that sharing. Others sometimes find it difficult to become sexually involved in such a casual way without feeling some sense of guilt. Still others would not even consider having quick sex with another. This is one of those areas you may want to spend some time thinking about in order to decide what your feelings and values are. One of the things that must be carefully considered is the increased risk of casual sex. When you do not have an established relationship of caring and trust, it is more difficult to be safe from the chances of disease transmission or emotional hurts.

In this chapter, we certainly should not lose sight of the fact that for many people who are working at the sharing of a loving relationship, sex is an important part of the sharing. People "in love" consistently report that a good sexual encounter often deepens their sense of communication with one another and indeed strengthens their love.

If you read back over the "Qualities of Being in Love," which were listed a few pages back, you may readily see how sex might fit into each of those qualities. People who share sexually in positive ways *choose* to do so with each other. The coming together of our bodies in sex certainly represents a *giving* of oneself and an unparalleled *closeness* and *delight* with another person. When we are together sexually with another human being, certainly the dimensions of *trust, caring, responsiblity,* and *respect* in our dealings with that person may be of the utmost importance. And as we share sex with someone else, we also increase our own *selfawareness;* we get closer to our own bodies and feelings and what they have to offer us.

However, it would be a mistake to assume that good sex is all there is to a good loving relationship. Likewise, it would be naive to believe that sexual contact with another person can only be fully

110 Sex and Sense

enjoyable and successful when loving feelings are involved. Each of us — as the individuals we are and want to be — must decide what the level of interaction between love and sex will be. There are no fast and ready rules that seem to apply successfully to everyone.

Jealousy and Possessiveness

When we have become very attached to another person, and feel that we love them intensely, we also may begin to fear that we will somehow lose them. It is scary to think that someone you love very deeply might eventually decide they do not want to be with you any longer. Nobody likes to feel rejected by another, especially a loved one. People who are in love naturally feel uncomfortable when the individual they love may seem interested in someone else, or is not as connected to the relationship as they would wish. It is natural to experience some of this feeling we call *jealousy*.

Jealousy is one of those things that couples need to be able to discuss and get out in the open. Otherwise, it can lead to resentment and other tensions in the relationship. However, jealousy sometimes gets out of control, and turns into a more serious problem of *possessiveness*. One partner may worry constantly about losing the other, and may even begin to imagine that the other person is straying into other relationships. The possessive person may become increasingly unreasonable, clinging, or demanding. He or she may seem desperate not to lose the loved partner and in turn may make the relationship all the more pressured and uncomfortable for that partner.

Sometimes jealousy and possessiveness grow out of personal insecurity. The individual may feel inadequate or insecure in other aspects of life, and those insecurities get played out in the loving relationship in the form of desperate possessiveness. Often, jealous and possessive people are not particularly willing to take full responsibility for changing their reactions and behaviors, and instead feel that their possessive feelings or actions are perfectly justified. These are signals that the person may be in need of counseling (see Chapter 7).

If you find yourself in a relationship with a person who seems unreasonably jealous, there are a few things you can do to make certain you are not being taken advantage of.

1. *Encourage the person to work on the jealousy.*
   You might even express a willingness to talk with a counselor together, after you have let the individual know that the jealousy is bothering you. Sometimes it is tempting just to give in to keep the peace, but this can become a continuing pattern that only leads to further trouble.

2. *Don't feel obligated to answer unreasonable questions or accusations.*
   If your partner seems convinced you are somehow failing the relationship, and grills you unreasonably about your possible interests in other people, don't fall into the trap of trying to defend yourself. Tell your partner instead how badly the questions make you feel, and stick with telling the truth. Again emphasize that you want the person to work on the jealous feelings.

3. *Don't let yourself be ruled by pity for the other person or by coercion.*
   Sometimes, you may even feel that you understand why your loved one is jealous or possessive. Or you may be frightened that if you do not give in to their demands, they might harm you or themselves. You must be very cautious in such situations. It is your partner's responsibility to work on personal problems, and your responsibility to protect yourself. Threats of one sort or another represent the kind of coercion that cannot lead to a healthy relationship. They mean it is time for you to seek help from someone you trust. (See pages 142–145 for suggestions on seeking help.)

4. *Think carefully about whether the relationship is right for you.*
   If jealousy or possessiveness seem to be getting out of control, it may be a sign that the relationship is headed in the wrong direction. You may want to assess carefully whether it

is a relationship in which you want to remain. Even if you care deeply for the other person, if their actions are constantly making you feel uncomfortable or controlled, you may need to think about ending the relationship for your own good.

Letting Go—When Relationships End

As much as we might not want to face it, loving relationships usually do not last forever. Most teenagers have more than one relationship that will be important to them. When people first fall in love, they are tempted to make promises that they will always stay together and always love one another. Such promises may simply not be very realistic. Eventually, people typically settle into a loving relationship with a more lasting commitment, but earlier relationships usually don't last forever.

People change, feelings change, and relationships change. Sometimes, it is simply time for a relationship to come to an end. Endings always hurt somewhat, especially after you have spent a great deal of time together. Yet, letting go of a relationship may be the best choice when one or both of the partners lack the desire and motivation to keep the commitment going. Promises or not, love holds no particular guarantees. It makes us vulnerable, and we sometimes have to accept the hurting that goes along with it.

When a relationship breaks up, there may be a mixture of emotions and reactions. There can be anger, sadness, and a deep sense of loss and grieving. There may also be some relief or a sense of readiness to move on to other relationships. Some people rush to get rid of their more painful feelings, but it can be important to experience them and deal with them as much as possible. Seeking out a counselor or trusted person to talk over your feelings often can help.

Ending relationships is as much a part of life as beginning them. Although it may feel for a time as though you will never want to allow yourself to love again, such feelings eventually pass. You can learn from every relationship you have, and then use that learning well when you establish a new loving relationship.

FORMING PARTNERSHIPS

When people are in love, they want to be together. In our society, people who are in love often want to form some sort of more formalized partnership. An obvious example of partnership is marriage, and surveys of college students indicate that about 96% of them intend to marry someday.

Cohabitation

Some couples live together, sharing sex, sharing the practical necessities of life, and developing strong loving commitments, without actually getting married. This sort of partnership is called *cohabitation*. Some of these relationships do not survive for long; others continue for years; and still others eventually lead to marriage. Census Bureau statistics for 1990 indicated that there were nearly three million unmarried couples living together in the United States—80% more than in 1980.

Some young people have assumed that living together prior to marriage is a good way to know one another better and to assure that the eventual marriage will be a success. They assume that during this trial period of cohabitation, they will be able to discover if they are not well suited for each other. Recent research suggests that this assumption is incorrect. In fact, a study of couples over many years indicates that cohabitation may actually increase the chances of divorce once the couple has married. This serves as another reminder that no matter what form a partnership takes, continuing to work at the relationship will be necessary.

Parents react in many different ways when they learn that an unmarried son or daughter is "living with" someone. I have seen the reaction in which parents are shocked and refuse to even speak to the son or daughter. Some parents decide that the relationship is acceptable but do not wish the couple to share the same bed when they come home for a visit. Other parents have no difficulty accepting the partnership. Many young couples who have decided to cohabitate have trouble deciding whether or not to tell their parents. Yet, they also find it difficult to predict their parents' reaction.

Changing Sex Roles

Healthy partnerships, whether married or unmarried, give both partners room to grow in directions of their own choosing. It is important for both of them to be independent individuals while sharing a relationship together. In the traditional marriage, it was sometimes impossible for the partners to be who they really were as individuals, or to find out about the best that each of them had to offer each other. Instead, they were busy doing what was expected of them as men or women.

Traditionally, a man was a person who worked to earn money for his family and acted as protector and businessman for family affairs. A woman traditionally took more responsibility for household tasks and raising children. As we began to explore in Chapter 3, traditional male-female roles have been changing, and that applies to marriages as well.

Current social trends are emphasizing the equality of women and men, and this influence is being felt in marriages and other partnerships. Many women find work outside the home enjoyable and fulfilling, and wish to contribute to the family financially. Likewise, men are taking over duties in the home, and are demonstrating patience and sensitivity in dealing with children. In other words, many couples are searching for the activities that feel right for them and that contribute to a happier partnership, without letting themselves be locked in unreasonable old patterns.

Partnerships and Successful Sex

Most couples want to develop a successful sexual relationship. First, I need to explain what I mean by "successful." It seems that a successful sexual relationship in a partnership includes the following qualities:

1. Both partners participate in choosing when to become involved sexually and do not feel manipulated or coerced into sex by the other.
2. Both partners generally find their sexual contacts to be pleasurable, satisfying, and desirable experiences.
3. Both partners usually feel satisfied that their bodies have functioned sexually as they wanted and that they are able to have orgasm when they wish.
4. There is some sense of freedom between the partners for variety and experimentation in their sexual activities, provided it is acceptable to both.
5. Neither partner feels pressured to participate in sexual activities that he or she does not find appealing or enjoyable.
6. Neither partner feels pressured to have sex when he or she does not wish to or solely for the other partner's enjoyment.

When people live together, they are bound to have more opportunity for sex. Likewise, the longer the two are together, the greater the likelihood for sexual problems—or an unsatisfactory sexual relationship—to develop. Like any other aspect of a healthy, growing partnership, sex takes some effort too.

It is important to remember, however, that most sexual problems cannot be worked out apart from the basic problems in the overall relationship. Part of working on these problems is that *good communication* I keep emphasizing. If one partner is feeling used, dissatisfied, or unhappy about sex or any other aspect of the relationship, but does not share the feeling with the other, things will probably not improve. *Compromise* is necessary in sex too. It is seldom that both partners are exactly alike in their sexual needs and preferences. In other words, your partner may not be interested in sex at the same times you are or may not enjoy the same kinds of sexual activity as you. Therefore, there will have to be compromises in both directions to develop a successful sexual relationship. In the sexual area and all others, compromise does not have to mean that you give up your own values or your own sense of individuality and self-worth. Many people believe that no relationship is worth preserving when sacrifices of this sort are required to sustain it.

THE MARRIAGE PARTNERSHIP

In recent years, attitudes toward marriage have been changing. I have heard many young people make statements such as: "I'll never get married!" "Marriage is just legalized sex." "Why get married when you can just live together!" "Marriage is out of date." In this section, we shall take a closer look at marriage in today's society and how sex fits into that picture. We shall also briefly examine other close partnerships between people that do not involve marriage.

The high rates of separation and divorce have been frightening some people. About 20% of people marrying today will be divorced within five years. Eventually, about 40% of marriages now taking place end in divorce, although there are many others that end in separation without divorce.

Of course, it is also important to note that changes in laws have made divorce much easier from a legal standpoint. The divorce statistics may not mean that the rate of unhappy, unsuccessful marriages has increased. Such marriages may simply now be easier to get out of, or more couples may be deciding that when communication stops—when love and caring, warmth and pride, cannot be sustained in a relationship—it is time to call it quits. In any case, plenty of marriages are not working. As this section points out, it is a step to be taken with care and planning.

Changing Patterns of Marriage

During past centuries, marriage among the wealthy classes was often a convenient business arrangement. Parents of daughters made arrangements with prospective husbands to give them a certain amount of property and money upon marriage. Often, the young people knew one another only slightly and certainly did not have a loving relationship. One important result of these marriages was children. The children made families even more powerful, as they carried on combined traditions and took their share of property and money.

Among the poorer, working classes a man would often seek a wife as a cook, housekeeper, and convenient partner for sex, again with little "love" between them. The children of these marriages were often considered status symbols — beings for a father (and to a lesser degree, a mother) to be proud of. The husband worked to provide money and shelter, while the wife fulfilled her duties in the home.

In some cultures today, marriages that are arranged by parents for convenience and property are still common. In nearly all of these cultures, it is the sons who share in the property of their families, whereas arrangements are made for daughters to marry, taking to their husbands smaller portions of their families' money or property.

Over the past 150 years, the predominant patterns of marriage have changed in most aspects of our society. One of the most significant changes has been the emphasis on marrying because of love for and commitment to another person. Gradually, it became important for a man and woman to spend time getting to know one another while their love grew and became stronger. Eventually the two might decide that they wanted to be married so that they could live together, share property, share sex, and raise a family. Marriage was the bond by which the government approved such a relationship and established certain legal responsibilities and limits for the two people. Usually, marriage included a religious ceremony in which the two people promised to uphold their religious customs and traditions as well.

Today, there are many differing points of view on what marriage should and should not be. Some people still hold traditional views, but others find them overly sentimental and unrealistic.

New Outlooks on Marriage

So why do people get married anyway? The answers to that question aren't simple as they once were. Many feel that a good case can be made for not being married as well. Nevertheless, a great many people are still marrying, for a great variety of reasons. Some very good marriages seem to grow out of foundations such as the following:

1. *Deepened commitment*

   Some couples who are working at love choose to formalize their commitment and establish a partnership as husband and wife. The marriage ceremony itself involves an exchange of vows between the partners—promises that two people make to one another. Today, it is very common for the two people to write their own vows—to decide what they are willing to promise. An important part of getting ready for marriage can be working out together what promises each individual is willing to make.

   Some people believe that the legal ties of marriage make it more difficult for married persons to simply leave their partners during rough times, instead of sticking with it and working on problems. Hopefully, however, a good marriage is based on a mutual commitment to work on difficulties, rather than a legal obligation to do so.

2. *Raising a family*

   Many couples decide to marry because they want to have children and feel that marriage provides a more socially acceptable environment in which to raise them. There is good evidence, too, that single parents can be very effective. Most professionals believe that there must be more in a good marriage than *just* the desire to have children. There must be a real commitment between two individuals who want to share many other aspects of their lives. More about being a parent in Chapter 9.

3. *Respect for tradition*

   Some people marry because they would not feel comfortable living together or having sexual intercourse without marriage. All of us must decide how important the values of our parents, religion, and society are to our own lives. Undoubtedly, some couples marry out of respect to parents or others, instead of living together without marrying. Such respect for tradition has its place, but no marriage is advisable until both partners have had a chance to understand what marriage means to them and to feel ready for it.

4. *Symbolizing fulfillment and security*

   As loving relationships develop, the individuals involved find more and more fulfillment and security in one another. One reason why many people marry is that they want to make a formal statement, symbolizing their desire to continue sharing with each other the many changing aspects of their lives. Healthy marriages give both the man and woman room to grow. They can both be individuals while sharing a relationship together.

5. *Practical considerations*

   In our society, people who are married are recognized as "next of kin," and this relationship gives them some special benefits that unmarried couples do not have. They may file joint income tax returns, automatically inherit each other's property, be included under employee health insurance plans, open joint bank accounts, and assume many other rights and privileges in relation to each other's lives.

Not Being Married

Marriage simply isn't for everyone. Some people either do not want or are not ready for either the formal or informal commitments, responsibilities, compromises, and problems that go with marriage. It is also a fact that many individuals live fulfilling, satisfying, happy lives without ever marrying.

Marriage during the teenage years is especially risky. Most professionals try to persuade teenagers either not to get married or to consider such a step with extreme caution. This is done with good reason, because over half of teenage marriages end in divorce. When most of those divorced couples married as teenagers, they were happy and quite convinced that their marriages would work. They were wrong. In the past, most people in the United States were married by the age of twenty-two. Gradually, that age is rising. The average marrying age for women is now twenty-four, and for men it is over twenty-six. It is generally accepted that a better time for most people to consider marriage is around the age of twenty-five or older.

Some couples marry for the wrong reasons. Here are some poor reasons, in themselves, for getting married.

1. *Sexual attraction*
   A marriage based on physical attraction alone will probably run into serious trouble eventually. A relatively small amount of time in marriage is spent in actual sexual contact. A physically attractive and sexually responsive partner may be a very desirable husband or wife, but other qualities must also be taken into consideration.

2. *To gain independence*
   Some people marry so that they can leave home and gain independence from their parents. Good marriages are usually the result of two partners who bring a certain type of independence to the marriage with them, and not a need to "escape" from home.

3. *Search for security*
   There are many different kinds of security people expect from marriage. But if you marry just for financial security, or for a convenient sexual partner, or out of fear of losing the other person, it is likely you will be disappointed by your marriage.

4. *Pressure from others*
   Americans place a high premium on marriage, and over 95%

of them marry at least once. Many unmarried young men and women in their early twenties begin to feel the pressure from a family and society that say, "Isn't it about time you were thinking about marriage and settling down?" As we have already stated, most people may not be ready for marriage until later in their lives, and some are never ready. Marriage should never happen just because "it's the thing to do."

5. *Unwanted pregnancy*

It is not unusual for a young couple to marry because they have started a pregnancy. If the pregnancy was not wanted, however, and one or both of the partners feel unprepared for the responsibilities of marriage and parenthood, the marriage is most likely a mistake. Creating an unhappy, unwilling marriage may not be the best or most responsible way to deal with a pregnancy or eventual parenthood.

6. *For status*

Some people marry out of the belief that they will "fit in" socially better if they have a spouse (husband or wife). Sometimes a marriage partner is chosen because he or she is attractive and looks like the "perfect" husband or wife. Such a superficial reason for marriage can hardly lead to lasting happiness or lifetime fulfillment.

Working at a Marriage

While organizing this section, I asked several people what they thought teenagers should know about marriage and other committed relationships. One twenty-four-year-old woman who remarried after her first marriage ended in divorce, put it like this:

Make sure they understand that a good marriage takes constant effort. Not just once in awhile, but day-in and day-out effort. It's not always fun, and it's certainly not always easy. But it's worth it.

Her thoughts were echoed by everyone else I talked to who had attempted a committed relationship with another person. The relationship and one's partner in it simply cannot be taken for granted. There must be a strong commitment to work at caring about each other and communicating with each other. That means being willing to take the other person's feelings, needs, and ideas into consideration along with your own. It also means working out the practical details of living together and taking care of cleaning, meals, and finances.

Two people are never exactly alike in their habits, interests, or goals for the future. In marriage, then, when two people live together and work toward a future together, there has to be *compromise*. That will mean that both partners must "give" a little, sometimes not doing things quite the way either of them alone might prefer. It may also mean that the two will sometimes get angry with one another. When that happens, good communication is really put to the test. If both can admit their feelings and deal with them as constructively as possible, then anger does not have to lead to destructive, hurtful name-calling that accomplishes little.

The Future of Marriage

Most experts agree that marriage—in some form or another —will be around for a long time. Statistics show that most divorced people remarry, and that more people are getting married than ever before.

Every decision to enter a partnership represents a contract. It is a contract between two human beings who are committing themselves to deeper levels of sharing. Each partner promises to participate in the positive and negative aspects of that commitment. Before taking the step toward marriage, it is important for both individuals to consider fully what that commitment means to their lives and exactly what kinds of promises they are ready to make to each other. Many couples could benefit from premarital counseling, so that they may talk through these important issues with a trusted counselor.

SOME VALUE QUESTIONS

As a way of helping you begin to think more fully about how sex and love will fit together for you, consider the following questions. Remember, there are no "right" and "wrong" answers —just *your* answers. And do not expect to find your answers in the next few minutes; they may be months or even years away.

1. Would you have sex with a person whom you have just met at a party and find physically attractive?
2. How do you feel about people who assure others that they love them, just so that they will have sex with them?
3. What kinds of qualities and feelings do you want to have in a relationship before you are ready to have a sexual contact with the other person?
4. What kind of loving relationships have you experienced in your life? How did sex become involved in those relationships? As you look back, how do you feel about the relationships?
5. Right now in your life, is there a person with whom you would be interested in sharing a sexual encounter? What kind of relationship do you have with this person? If the opportunity for sex comes along, what do you think you will do?
6. Do you or could you love a member of your own sex? If so, how is this different from or the same as the love you might feel for a member of the opposite sex?
7. What have your parents, school, and religious group taught you about the relationship of sex and love? How important to you are these teachings?

Partnerships and Your Life

1. Think about the following questions and decide where you stand right now in your life. During the next few years, some

of your values may change, but try to focus in on what you believe at present.

(a) Do you expect to marry someday? Why or why not?

(b) Of the married couples you know, which have the relationship(s) that seem most appealing to you? Think about those couples:

What are the characteristics of each individual that seem to make the marriages "work"?

(c) How important do you think sex should be in a marriage?

2. What kind of partner do you want?

(a) Consider the following list of personal qualities and characteristics. Pick out the ten that seem most important to you in a partner:

Good-looking face
Attractive body
Good cook
Intelligent
Good education
Gentle and kind
Has plenty of money
Honest and sincere
Unemotional and controlled
Places few demands on you
Likes travel and excitement
Good housekeeper
Independent spirit
Quiet and a little shy
Enjoys parties and
    entertaining
Has same interests as you

Likes children
Has a good job
Good sex partner
Dependent on you
Gets along well with others
Less intelligent than you
Wants a nice home
Will allow you sexual
    freedom
Aggressive go-getter
Wants to communicate
Shows emotions
Has different interests
Does not want children
Wants a simple life
Other: _____
_____

(b) Now, think about the ten qualities you have chosen. Assign them each a number from 1 to 10, 1 being the most important to you, and 10 being the least important to you.

1. _____   6. _____
2. _____   7. _____
3. _____   8. _____
4. _____   9. _____
5. _____   10. _____

For Further Reading

Calderone, Mary S. and Eric W. Johnson. *The Family Book About Sexuality*. Scranton, Pennsylvania: HarperCollins, 1990.

Douglas, J. D. and F. C. Atwell. *Love, Intimacy, and Sex*. Newbury Park, California: Sage Publications, 1990.

Kelly, Gary F. *Sexuality Today: The Human Perspective*. Guilford, Connecticut: Dushkin Publishing Group, 1992.

7 Communicating About Sex and Sexual Problems

As a counselor who talks with other people about their feelings and concerns, I am continually reminded of how important good communication really is in human relationships. Yet, I have also discovered that many individuals have a great deal of misunderstanding about how to establish lines of communication.

FUNDAMENTALS OF GOOD COMMUNICATION

I have come to believe that there are three important foundations that must be established before people can communicate with each other with full effectiveness. Those three foundations are as follows:

1. *A sense of equality*
   Both individuals must feel a sense of equality with one another and as good, worthwhile people in their own rights. There cannot be an underlying belief that one person is

"better" than the other. Little productive two-way communication can take place if one of the individuals feels judged, put-down, or preached at by the other. Such feelings often lead to defensiveness and pointless argument. So, for effective communication to take place, both people must be willing to be open to the other's ideas, opinions, and feelings, even though there may be disagreement over them. It is important to remember that people communicate in different ways. One partner in a relationship, for example, may have a better capacity to find the truth in a situation and clarify the scope of a problem. The other partner may more easily discover the right thing to do in a situation, and put decisions into action. Equality in a relationship doesn't mean that people have only the same things to contribute.

2. *The desire to communicate*
    If fear, stubbornness, lack of caring, or some other block gets in the way of one person's desire to communicate, it is not likely that much is going to happen. There are many reasons why people may desire to communicate. Among those reasons are a desire to improve the relationship; inner discomforts that need to be talked out; tension between the two people to be dealt with; or simply knowing the joy that real communication may yield.

3. *Working at it*
    Good two-way communication takes energy. It is always a bit risky because sharing openly with another person leaves us more vulnerable than before. So, work—expenditure of energy—is necessary. Like any other kind of work, we sometimes have to make the effort to communicate even when we're not quite in the mood.

I hope that these three basic rules do not seem overwhelming to you. However, the unavoidable fact is that good communication between human beings is not a simple matter; it doesn't "just happen." It grows out of human foundations.

What Gets Communicated and How?

What kinds of things get communicated from person to person? Here is a list of some of the most important elements of communication:

1. Thoughts and ideas
2. Feelings
3. Values, attitudes, and opinions
4. Needs and desires

All of these things may be communicated to another person. They are conveyed in a great variety of ways, some of the most common of which are:

1. *Using words*
   A great deal of communication occurs through the use of words, either spoken or on paper.
2. *Eye contact*
   It is said that the eyes are the mirrors of the soul. There certainly can be some important messages communicated by the amount of eye contact two people have.
3. *Facial expression*
   Our faces are particularly important in communication. Even when we hear words from another individual, we often scan his or her face, searching for the true meaning behind the words.
4. *Body movements and contact*
   The manner in which our body moves also conveys messages to others. A particularly intense form of communication involves one person physically touching another.

Misunderstandings and Games

A big problem with communication is that one person often does not fully understand the other person's exact meaning, or the meaning may be completely misinterpreted. This is one of the reasons why good communication takes so much work. It is essential to stay really in touch with what another person is saying and sometimes we have to ask questions in order to understand the whole message. Often, we are too busy thinking about what we ourselves are going to say next to really listen.

Sometimes people substitute games and deceptions for good communication. Getting caught up in games can happen easily, and some individuals find it simpler to play the game than to strive for open, honest, two-way communication. For more selfish reasons, communication may also become deceitful manipulation of another person. This is a dangerous kind of communication because it is almost certain to produce further misunderstandings and hurt.

SEX AND COMMUNICATION

One of the very important areas about which people often need to communicate is sexuality. Most of what we learn about sex is communicated to us by other people. Yet sex is also an area that creates feelings that can block good communication. When the subject of sex comes up, some people feel embarrassed, ashamed, afraid, or even angry. Instead of being able to communicate those feelings, they may try to avoid the whole subject. Some individuals also hold very strong values and attitudes about sex and do not care to hear from others who might not agree with them. Consequently, sex often just doesn't get talked about.

There is one important suggestion that I give to people who want to improve lines of communication about sex (or anything) with someone else. It is to try to present honestly just *what you are feeling*. We can really only guess what is going on with the other person anyway, so it is dangerous to make assumptions. Sometimes, it is even difficult to know exactly what we ourselves are feeling. Here is an illustration of some poor communication, showing what is really going on and also how the communication could have been improved by being honest about feelings:

What was said:	What was being thought:	What could have been said:
Ed: "I heard you went out with Rick last night."	(How come you didn't call me last night?)	"I was kind of hoping we could go somewhere together last night, but I heard you went out with Rick."
Sue: "Yeah, Ann and I went to the movies, and Rick happened to be there too. So, he sat with us."	(I wonder why he sounds so mad? How come he didn't call me if he wanted to see me so much?)	"I was hoping you would call me. But then Ann called and we went to the movies. Rick just happened to sit with us."
Ed: (sarcastically) "Did you have a good time?"	(Maybe she enjoyed being with him more than she would have with me.)	"When I heard you were with him, I felt really kind of hurt and confused."
Sue: (defensively) "So what if I did? I have a right to do what I want to do."	(Doesn't he trust me?)	"I'm sorry you were hurt. I guess we both should have tried to get together last night."
Ed: "I thought we were going steady."	(I'm afraid I'm losing her.)	"Probably. But sometimes I worry that you are getting sick of having me around."
Sue: "That doesn't mean you own me."	(Sometimes he makes me feel so trapped!)	"I'm not sick of you at all. I worry about the same thing. But maybe sometimes we need to spend time apart. That doesn't mean we care about each other less."
Ed: (angrily) "Well, if you want to break up, just tell me."	(I don't want this to happen, but maybe she's sick of me.)	"Yeah, but sometimes I get scared of losing you."
Sue: (frustrated) "That's not what I meant."	(Why does he always bring that up? Probably he's the one who wants to break up.)	"I don't even like to think about breaking up with you."

The kind of communication that Ed and Sue exhibited is typical of the misunderstandings and second-guessing games that go on between people all the time. Yet, this poor communication may be turned into positive, productive communication by remembering to stop second-guessing the other person and to share your own thoughts and feelings to the greatest extent you feel able. To be sure, that kind of openness leaves us vulnerable, and some people take advantage of others' vulnerability. But most will respond by sharing their thoughts and feelings, and then two-way communication is underway.

Talking with Parents About Sex

When it comes to sex, don't sell your parents short. Keep in mind that they are sexual people too and may have many worthwhile things to share with you. Some parents find it easy to talk with their kids about sex, whereas others are extremely uncomfortable with the subject. If you're interested in their ideas and values concerning sexuality, it may be up to you to initiate the discussion. It is also good to remember that very little may be accomplished if the discussion turns into an argument. When there is disagreement, it is best to try to see the other's point of view and try to understand it as *different,* not wrong. The same rules for productive communication apply in families too. Instead of second-guessing what the other person is feeling and thinking, try to convey as honestly as possible what you are feeling and thinking. With parents, as well as others with whom you attempt to communicate, it's important to know when to stop trying to communicate. If values and attitudes are set, and unlikely to change, it may sometimes be best just to accept this.

Sex Education

In recent years, there have been many controversies about sex education. Actually, sex education of one sort or another goes on around us all the time. It begins when we are born. From the moment we are assigned our status as boy or girl, we are taught to think and act about our sexuality in very specific ways. We are sometimes dressed in blue or pink and given toys considered appropriate for boys and girls. As we progress through childhood, we learn many attitudes toward our bodies and sex from our parents. Usually by late childhood, we have learned to feel positively or negatively about our sex organs and our sexual feelings.

Our families are one of our most important sources of sex education, even into adulthood. Our peers—people our own age—often are significant sources of information about sex. More and more, schools and religious groups are offering sex education programs to young people and sometimes to adults. A full program in sex education consists of two aspects: (1) facts about our bodies and how they function sexually (this is what I usually call the "plumbing") and (2) opportunity to talk about sexual feelings and values with peers and adults.

Sex education in public schools must allow for a free exchange of facts and values, rather than adherence to a single point of view. Church or synagogue programs are legitimate places for the teaching of particular religious or moral values concerning sex. Parents, too, usually want to convey to their children the moral values in which they believe. If you ever become a parent, some of the responsibility for educating your children about sex will be yours.

Sex education is a lifelong process. Throughout our lives we continue to learn about our own sexuality and about the facts of sex. There are many books now available and many more yet to appear that can help people to understand human sexuality more fully. Choose your books with care, however, and beware of those which promise to erase effortlessly all of your sexual concerns and inhibitions.

Communication and Healthy Sexual Relationships

One of the most dangerous areas for games, deceptions, and misunderstandings is sex. In a healthy, growing relationship where sexual feelings are involved in any way, communication may be of extreme importance. Attention must continually be given to what is going on between two people sexually: Is one person feeling guilty, or trapped, or inadequate? Is sex being used as an escape or a cover-up of negative feelings? Are both partners happy and satisfied with what they are doing sexually?

Earlier in this chapter, there was an example of some poor communication between Ed and Sue as they discussed their relationship. The same kinds of miscommunication can happen when two people talk about sex. Here is how Ed and Sue tried to communicate about sex in their relationship.

What was said:	What was being thought:	What could have been said:
Sue: "Whenever we're alone, you're all over me."	(Sometimes I think he only enjoys being with me when we're alone.)	"I really need to talk about how I feel when we're alone like this."
Ed: (sarcastically) "I suppose you don't like it."	(What's going on? I thought this is what she wanted me to do.)	(curiously) "Okay, what's going on?"
Sue: "What's that supposed to mean—I'm easy?"	(I wonder what he does think about me.)	"I've just been wondering how you feel about me lately. Sometimes I think you just like being with me for sex."
Ed: "Everbody else is doing it. Why shouldn't we?"	(What's wrong with her all of the sudden?)	"I've been feeling kind of the same way. I'm confused about the whole thing."
Sue: "Is that all I am? Another conquest to brag about to your friends?"	(Sometimes he makes me feel so used.)	"I guess we never thought very much about what sex would mean to us."
Ed: "If that's what you think I guess you don't know me very well."	(I thought she knew how we felt about each other.)	"It means a lot to me, but nothing is more important than how we feel toward each other."
Sue: "No, I guess I don't anymore, since we started having sex."	(I don't think he cares about me anymore except for sex.)	"I'm glad you feel that way too."

Good communication about sex also takes honesty and openness about feelings. When two people can avoid accusations, and can share fears, needs, and concerns instead, there is a much greater likelihood that they will improve their sexual relationship rather than harm it.

Another essential part of a healthy sexual relationship is compromise. Neither partner can have things exactly his or her own way all the time. There must be compromises in both directions, and there cannot be meaningful compromise without good communication and mutual caring. Both people must share thoughts, feelings, preferences, and needs, and then care enough about one another to find the kind of sexual sharing that will be enjoyable, fulfilling, satisfying, and fair to both.

COPING WITH SEXUAL PROBLEMS

When does sex become a problem? It may be a problem in many different ways for many different people. It is probably safe to assume that almost all people have a sex-related problem or concern at some time in their lives. Such problems may last for a lifetime if not dealt with adequately, or they may disappear easily after a very short time.

There are several ways in which sexual feelings or activities may become a problem. Here are some of those ways:

1. When they produce guilt, fear, or negative attitudes about oneself.
2. When another person's right to privacy is violated or a law is broken.
3. When one person does not consider personal responsibility toward another and uses sexual deception or manipulation.
4. When someone is emotionally or physically harmed by the feelings or activities.
5. When the body does not function as expected or desired.
6. When an unwanted pregnancy occurs. (See Chapter 9.)
7. When a disease is transmitted by the sexual contact.

What People Worry About

As a counselor and sex therapist, I have talked with many individuals about their sexual worries. Some of those individuals mistakenly believed that they were the *only* ones who have had their particular worry. Actually, their concerns are usually quite typical. That does not make the problem any less troublesome, however. One of the most common worries is about *bodily development*. Boys and men often dislike their general physical appearance or believe their penises to be undersized. Sometimes, they are embarrassed enough to avoid swimming or other situations where they might be even partially unclothed. Likewise, girls and women are particularly prone to worry about their breast development, as well as general physical appearance.

Messages from our society can foster even more worry about our bodies. The people portrayed in pictures for advertisements, and in other media, tend to have bodies that are particularly perfect. It is easy to get the impression that these perfect bodies are the average, and it is also easy to imagine that the rest of us are hardly measuring up to that perfection. Again, it is important to keep in mind that human bodies, and their various organs, come in many different shapes and sizes, all perfectly normal. Most of us are just never going to look like a model, and the less energy we waste on trying to do so, the more we'll have for being the best possible person we can be in our own right.

Masturbation is another typical concern of people at all ages. People often wonder if they are masturbating too much or what the effects of masturbation may be. Usually accurate information can clear up many of these worries and doubts. Masturbation was discussed in detail in Chapter 3. People also worry about the *daydreams* and *fantasies* they may have while masturbating or just thinking about sex. They sometimes fear that their fantasies mean that they are "weird." Actually, most people occasionally think about some sexual practices that they may choose never to become involved in. For example, it is not unusual to daydream about sexual involvement with another person of either sex, a teacher, or a stranger who is sexually attractive. You do not have to do what you think about. It will be up to you to decide whether doing any of the things you daydream about corresponds with your basic preferences and values.

Many young people who become involved in close relationships find their sexual worries increasing if they begin dating or sharing loving feelings. Both boys and girls wonder if they should initiate sex play with their dating partners and wonder how to go about making such advances. Early attempts at sexual contact may be awkward and embarrassing, and that only leads to further worry. If sex play is begun, then there may be further concern about "how far to go." If the relationship begins to involve intensive sexual activity, then it is possible for many new problems to develop. People may be concerned about possible exposure to H.I.V. or other diseases. They may face *guilt* or other negative feelings after sex, and following heterosexual intercourse, there is often a *fear of pregnancy*. Another common concern is that one has *too much or too little* "sex drive," or that one is not *"performing"* in sex as well as possible.

Those young people who become involved in relationships with members of their same sex may find their sexual worries increasing. They not only have the same problems in making relationships and knowing when sex is appropriate, but other worries as well. They may have loving feelings for people whom they would not dare tell. They may have to hide the fact that they are "dating" or experimenting with sex. Though many colleges and some high schools now have gay social organizations, and some larger communities have gay youth groups, young people who are gay or lesbian often have a difficult time finding ways to meet other gay people in a congenial setting that is suitable for building relationships. Due to the attitudes in our society about homosexuality, young people who embark on same sex relationships may have even greater problems with guilt. Young men and women who are experiencing guilt about homosexual feelings must ask themselves whether or not this guilt is justified by their own values and lifestyle choices. It may be desirable to talk over such concerns with a counselor (see pages 142–145). If you would like to find out more about gay organizations in your area, you might contact one of the organizations listed in Appendix II.

So these concerns represent very typical sexual worries of human beings. There are no magic solutions or easy answers that will make such worries disappear. Each of us must sort through his or her own conflicts, feelings, and values, searching for the lifestyle and sexual choices that fit best. Sometimes, it helps to talk over our worries with a trusted person, as discussed later in this chapter.

Sex and People with Disabilities

People with disabilities often have their own special sex-related problems. Attitudes toward various disabilities are filled with misunderstanding and prejudice. For example, it is often assumed that anyone with a disability does not, or should not, have sexual feelings and needs. Yet all human beings, even those with severe physical impairments, are sexual beings as well.

When you are not used to being around someone who is visually or hearing impaired, it is natural to feel somewhat awkward and uncomfortable. It is difficult to know exactly how to communicate. Young people who are visually or hearing impaired often feel very isolated and frustrated because others may be hesitant to enter into relationships with them. Early ventures into love and sex are difficult enough, and facing others' discomfort because of a disability only magnifies fears and self doubts. Sex education must sometimes be modified for teenagers with disabilities. Three-dimensional models of sex organs and other body parts are used for those with visual impairments. Young people with hearing impairments may need to practice appropriate ways of communicating that will be understandable and nonthreatening to others.

People with cerebral palsy or injury to their spinal cords may have difficulty controlling their muscular movements or may be partially paralyzed. Nevertheless, they still may desire sexual activity, and there are always ways of arranging suitable positions and special accommodations for most forms of sex to take place. Even individuals who are paralyzed in the region of their sex organs can participate in sex. Men often are still capable of erection and even ejaculation, whereas women may still achieve vaginal lubrication, with direct stimulation of the sex organs. The extent to which the sex organs still respond during sexual stimulation depends on the nature and extent of a spinal cord injury or disease. Many people who have become paralyzed report having learned a lesson that most of us could pay more attention to: that sex can be, and should be, far more than what our penises and vaginas can do.

Young people who have some form of mental disability may not be seen as sexual people either, even though they also have sexual needs and feelings. It is particularly important for them to be given patient attention and sex education that is done in ways they can comprehend, so that they will learn how to manage their sexual feelings and behaviors in socially acceptable ways. They must also learn how to protect themselves from being sexually exploited by others.

The message from young people with disabilities is clear: See us as people with the same hopes, fears, interests, and problems as everyone else. Give us a chance. Recognize us as sexual human beings who need love, closeness, and touching just like you.

Sexual Exploitation

Exploitation refers to taking advantage of other people or "abusing" them. There is plenty of exploitation in many forms of irresponsible sex. Anytime that an individual is persuaded to become involved in sex through trickery or deceit, exploitation is going on. If one partner is interested primarily in selfish physical pleasure, but pretends that sex is a loving and spiritual thing, exploitation is going on. Sexual abuse is discussed in more detail in Chapter 10.

When Sex Doesn't Work

Sometimes our sex organs do not function quite the way we want or expect them to. Occasionally, that may be due to a lack of sexual excitement, so that the body does not begin its sexual response cycle (see p. 45). Other times, we may feel sexually aroused and be interested in reaching orgasm, but our bodies simply do not respond as expected.

Most people discover from time to time that their sex organs do not respond as they want. This is normal and may be expected occasionally. Individuals should try to accept such occasional problems without undue worry, criticism, or embarrassment—in themselves and in their sexual partners. In fact, worrying about them sometimes only increases the frequency of problems. If a person's sex organs *consistently* do not function as he or she wants—and the person is not being misled by exaggerated expectations from movies or novels—then it may be advisable to seek professional advice from a qualified sex therapist. Here are some of the difficulties that men and women may face, sometimes called sexual dysfunctions:

At some point in their lives, most men have a sexual experience in which they cannot get an erection of the penis or cannot keep the erection long enough to have orgasm. This is sometimes called *impotence*. Fatigue, depression, and consumption of alcohol may lead to temporary erection difficulties. Some men are troubled by impotence for long periods of time. This problem often is caused by psychological factors, although physical conditions may be involved. It often goes away by itself, especially with an understanding and loving sexual partner, or—if serious enough—may be helped by sex therapy.

Men may also be concerned about reaching orgasm too rapidly—sometimes within a few seconds after intense sexual activity has begun. This is called *lack of ejaculatory control* or *premature ejaculation,* and is sometimes unsatisfying not only for the man but for his partner. This often occurs in young men who are highly excited during their first sexual experiences and also in men who have *learned* to reach orgasm rapidly during masturbation. They may also be helped to re-learn techniques for delaying their ejaculation and for making sex more enjoyable for their partners. Learning how to slow down during masturbation is one technique used. Another difficulty is *delayed ejaculation,* in which the man finds it difficult or impossible to reach orgasm, even though he has no problems maintaining an erection. This can be very frustrating and may require professional advice.

Some women and men find it difficult to become sexually aroused and are generally uninterested in sexual contact. This may be a sign that they simply do not want sex at that time and need to wait until such a decision feels all right. It may also signal deeper problems in need of professional attention. Some women also become sexually aroused, but have *difficulty reaching orgasm.* It should be understood, however, that interest in sex varies with different individuals, and in our culture many women and men are not especially interested in reaching orgasm each time they have sex. For anyone concerned about lack of interest in sex or trouble reaching orgasm, sex therapy can help.

A few women experience a problem called *vaginismus,* in which the vaginal muscles tighten so that sexual intercourse, or other forms of sexual activity in which vaginal penetration is made, can become painful or even impossible. (As mentioned in an earlier chapter, the male penis does not ever become "caught" in the vagina, however.) This dysfunction is also caused by psychological stress and may be helped by appropriate therapy.

Many of the problems discussed in this section are caused by anxiety about sex and the fear of not living up to one's own or a partner's expectations. They may also be caused by tensions and pressures that are not related to sex at all, but to stresses and misunderstandings in other areas of a relationship. In any case, these problems may be helped or prevented by working for healthy, guilt-free, relaxed relationships between loving, responsible individuals who care about one another's feelings—relationships in which sex is only a part. When problems do arise, however, it may be desirable to work on what might be getting in the way of effective communication between the partners, rather than concentrating on the sexual area right away. When sexual dysfunctions persist, they may be helped by learning particular techniques that help people become more relaxed and comfortable with sex. This may require the services of a competent, professional sex therapist. Some of the organizations listed in Appendix II (p. 255) may be able to help. There are a number of sex therapy clinics at large medical centers in North America that can also give advice, counseling, and treatment, although the cost of such services may be too steep for many young people to afford.

Preventing Problem Sex

Even though sex-related problems occur at some point in nearly everyone's life, there are some suggestions that may help prevent at least some problems. Suggestions have been given elsewhere in this book, but a summary follows:

1. *Willingness to be honest*
   Honesty with oneself and with potential sex partners. What are you really feeling, and what are you really looking for in sex? Is sex something you really want right now for your life, or for your relationship with someone you love?
2. *Becoming comfortable with your own sexuality*
   Many problems arise out of dissatisfaction with one's own sexual preferences and behaviors. To become comfortable with your sexuality, learn more about sex through books and courses, and spend some time thinking about what is sexually interesting and uninteresting for you. Then ask yourself whether the things you are doing or not doing sexually are the result of your own choices. Have you been doing what

you think you are "supposed" to do or what you think other people—including your sexual partner—"expect" of you? You may want to talk about sex with a good counselor.

3. *Good communication*
   Discussions with friends and people you love can prevent many sex problems. If you cannot talk openly about sex and your feelings with someone you love, or about such practical problems as hygiene or birth control, you are probably not ready for responsible sex with that person.

4. *Being realistic about sex*
   Don't try to model yourself or your sexuality after someone you have read about or have seen in movies or on television. Be yourself and find your own sexuality. Remember that sex is not always spectacular. Not placing unrealistic sexual expectations on yourself or your partner will allow you both the freedom to be yourselves sexually.

5. *Maintaining a sense of responsibility*
   Responsibility toward self and others is also essential to prevention of sex problems. Responsible sex does not lead to unwanted pregnancy, spread of sexually transmitted diseases, or the hurting of oneself or others. Caring about life and people carries with it important responsibilities.

6. *Knowing when to seek help*
   As much as we like to feel independent and in-control of situations, some problems simply cannot be dealt with alone. Sometimes if we neglect to get proper outside help, the problem simply grows and becomes even more troublesome or dangerous. Knowing when and how to seek appropriate help can prevent most problems from getting worse.

Finding a Counselor

To whom do you talk when you have a problem or have something you need to think through with another person? Whether it is to talk about sex or any other aspect of our lives, most of us sometimes feel the need to share some thoughts and feelings with another person. Perhaps you already know who that person would be for your life: a parent, a brother or sister, a counselor, a teacher, a member of the clergy, your best friend, a grandparent, or another relative. But what happens if you just don't know whom you should choose? What kind of individual do you search for? In this section, I will describe some of the things that seem to be important for me and many other people in finding someone to talk with.

First, be careful not to look for someone to solve your problems for you and make decisions for you. If you take time to think and feel and talk about what is going on, you will be able to find your own directions for your life. So look for someone who will not be too anxious to jump in and run things for you; someone who will be able to give you the freedom and responsibility to live your own life while giving you support, understanding, and the new perspective that another human being may have to offer. I wish I could say that if you seek out a counselor or doctor or psychologist you will automatically find such a person, but this is not always the case. Professional qualifications do not guarantee the presence of the right personal qualities that you may need in another. Likewise, many individuals without special training may be very good people to share things with.

Here are some of the qualities you might want to have in a person with whom you are going to talk:

1. *Trust*
   It is always important to feel trust for the person, knowing that what you talk about will be held in confidence and that your best interests will be foremost in that person's mind.

2. *Respect*
   Most people prefer to talk with others whose own lives seem worthy of respect. Although we cannot expect perfection from others, I usually appreciate talking with someone who is always working at being happy and at getting things straight for his or her own life.

3. *Caring*

How important it is to know that the other person can really care for you enough to want to share some thoughts and feelings with you! If he or she does not take your concerns very seriously, then look for someone who will.

4. *No quick judgments*

It seems that we make the best progress when the other person is not too quick to make judgments about what is going on. Look for a good listener who can sift through all aspects of the situation with you without coming to any quick conclusions or instant solutions.

5. *Empathy*

This refers to the ability to understand what other people are really feeling and being able to some degree to feel it along with them. It is an essential quality for a good counselor.

6. *Genuineness*

It is important for most people to talk with someone who is willing to share some of his or her own life as well; someone who will care enough to show feelings and thoughts, even if they are not quite what we might want to hear. Yet, it is important that any sharing is done in a real spirit of caring.

7. *Understanding*

We need to talk with people who will work to understand what we mean as closely as possible. With so much opportunity for misunderstanding in human communication, good counselors are always making certain that they understand what is being said to the best of their abilities.

How you might go about finding the right person for you to talk with will have to be up to you. It is always possible to ask someone you trust to suggest a good counselor for you, but the final decision should be your own. Some of the organizations listed on pages 256-259, or their local affiliates, may be able to offer some help. If you are talking with someone you did not know beforehand, it may take more than one session before you can be certain whether or not this is the right person for you. Remember:

it is usually scary to take that first step—to talk over some deeply personal things with someone else, especially if you do not know that person well.

Don't expect counselors to pick things out of your head. They too have to rely on honest, open communication to understand what is going on with another person. If you have spent some time talking with a counselor, really working at sharing yourself with him or her, and you still feel uncomfortable, then it would be wise to tell the counselor how you are feeling. Good counselors will help you to sort through your feelings so that you feel more comfortable talking with them or they will help you find someone else who is better for you. Keep in mind that you have the right to look for another counselor if you have not found the right one for yourself.

COMMUNICATION AND YOU

1. *Letters to Mom and Dad*
   (a) Here are two letters that young people gave me when I asked them to write what they would like to be able to tell their parents. Their parents never actually read the letters, and the two teenagers never got around to talking these things over with them. Read the two letters carefully and think about them. How do you feel about the people who wrote them? Do they sound at all like things you would like to tell your parents?

Dear Mom and Dad,

There are so many things I wish I could tell you. For one thing, why don't you trust me anymore? You don't seem to like some of my friends very much, but I don't really think you have given yourselves a chance to get to know them. They're good kids, really!

Sometimes, I lie to you about what I'm doing. When I tell you I'm going to the library or the movies, I'm usually riding around with some kids or hanging around a dorm at the college. I don't do anything wrong, but if I told you the truth, you would probably think the worst. I hate lying to you, but I don't know what else to do. Please try to understand me at least a little.

Your daughter,
Marie (age 16)

Dear Mom and Dad,

There is only one way to start this—just jump in. I want to talk to you about sex. That's right: S-E-X. I've never heard much about it from you, but I've managed to find out quite a bit for myself. I started masturbating seven years ago, and I've already had intercourse a few times.

The thing is, I still don't know what I want with sex. So far, it hasn't been too great, and it has hurt a lot of feelings. Sometimes, I even worry that I might be a little queer. So I need to talk about sex, and I don't know how. I feel like I have a lot more to learn. Can you help?

Your confused son,
Sam (age 16)

(b) Now, try writing your own "Dear Mom and Dad" letter. Sit down with a piece of paper and write those things that you would like to say to them. Perhaps you will write to just one parent, or maybe there is someone else to whom you would like to write a letter. Remember, you don't have to send the letter.

2. *Dealing with anger*

Try to recall the last two or three times when you got angry with another person. Remember the incidents in as much detail as possible, then consider the following aspects of each incident:

(a) How did you express your anger? Did you yell, fight, cry, or sulk? Did you store it up inside and pretend you weren't angry?

(b) Now, try to look beneath your anger. Is there a possibility that the other person *hurt* you in some way? Very often, when our feelings get hurt, we react with anger. How might you have been hurt?

(c) If you were hurt, try to imagine what might have happened if you had told the other person that he or she hurt you, instead of getting angry. Could that have worked for you and perhaps even strengthened your relationship with that person?

(d) Next time you begin to feel anger, try to stop and take a look at what you are really feeling. Try to share that with the other person and talk out what you both feel. It may be a step toward productive communication. (It is difficult to talk when you are really angry, though, so ironing out problems may sometimes have to wait until you've calmed down. Also, if a person you are trying to deal with *always* seems to get angry, or to make you angry, that may be a sign that he or she is a person you just cannot communicate with.)

3. *Communication and sex*

(a) Here is a list of topics relating to sex that may concern you in some way. Check which people you feel able to talk with about each topic at this point in your life (you may want to use a separate paper):

I can talk about this with:

Topics	A Parent	A Brother or Sister	A Good Friend	A Counselor	No One
Masturbation	_____	_____	_____	_____	_____
Sexual intercourse	_____	_____	_____	_____	_____
Homosexuality	_____	_____	_____	_____	_____
My sexual feelings	_____	_____	_____	_____	_____
My body and sex organs	_____	_____	_____	_____	_____
What I have done sexually	_____	_____	_____	_____	_____
My sexual worries	_____	_____	_____	_____	_____
Premarital sex	_____	_____	_____	_____	_____

(b) Now, look at your check marks. Are there more check marks in some columns than others? What do your marks tell you about your relationship with others?

(c) Are you satisfied with the patterns that your check marks have taken? Would you like to improve your communication with other people about sex? If so, begin to think about how you might accomplish that. It may be easier than you think. It may also be harder than you think, especially if the other person is not ready to meet you half way. Remember, both parties must be willing to communicate, and it's important to choose people who are as willing to be open as you are.

PROBLEM SEX AND YOUR LIFE

The following exercises can move you toward a better understanding of your values concerning certain sexual problems and encourage you to think about the avenues for help that you know about.

1. *What would you suggest?*
Consider each of the following sex-related problems. If a good friend brought the problem to you, what suggestions would you have for your friend? Keep in mind that you are not expected to help resolve the problem all by yourself, but only to suggest some ways in which the friend could find help.
In a classroom setting, each of these situations can be role-played aloud, with other members of the class commenting on the result and making further suggestions.
(a) A boy confides to you that he is worried about a burning feeling when he urinates. Two weeks before, he had sexual intercourse with a girl who is a friend of yours. It was his first sexual experience and he feels guilty about it.
(b) A girl telephones and hesitantly tells you that a boy with whom she recently had sexual intercourse just told her that he may have some sort of infection. She is upset and frightened and asks for your advice.
(c) A boy tells you that another boy in the class has suggested to him that they have homosexual sex. He is very frightened

of and opposed to homosexuality, and he feels very angry and insulted, as if his manhood has been challenged. He is planning some way to hurt the boy who made the suggestion to him.

(d) A girl tells you that she thinks she is in love with another girl, her best friend. She thinks the other girl may feel the same way, but she is frightened to talk with her about it. If her friend is disgusted, and she is rejected, she knows she will never be able to stand it. If her friend does feel the same way, she might not be able to handle it either, because she herself is very nervous about the idea of being "homosexual."

2. *Your worries*

(a) After thoroughly reading this chapter, read through the following list and note which of the items you have been concerned or upset about—either as a part of your own life or the life of someone close to you. Also, pick the one or two that have been the biggest problem(s) for you:

masturbation	lack of interest in sex
homosexual feelings	being sexually abused
sexual fantasies and dreams	sexually transmitted disease
the size or shape of your sex organs	erection difficulty
	lack of ejaculatory control
the size or development of your body	inability to have an orgasm
	vaginismus
"how far to go" sexually	inability to become sexually aroused
guilt about sex	
fear of pregnancy	risks of getting AIDS

(b) Now consider those items that you have considered to be sex-related problems for your life. How did you handle the problems? If the problem is still with you, are you doing anything about it? Should you be seeking some sort of outside help to deal with the problem? If you feel the need to work on a sexual problem, why not *design a plan of action right now?* Here are some questions to think about that may help in thinking through your design:

_____ Do you have adequate information about your problem?

_____ Do you know if other people—including professional counselors—would consider your "problem" to be truly a problem?

_____ Is the problem one that requires medical help, and, if so, where can you find a physician, nurse, or other medical professional whom you trust and can talk to?

_____ Should you talk about the problem with a counselor?

_____ Do you sometimes think that you are the only person who has this problem? You can be sure that many others share the same problem.

For Further Reading

Finger, Anne. *Past Due: A Story of Disability, Pregnancy, and Birth.* Seattle, Washington: The Seal Press, 1990.

Glass, Lillian. *He Says, She Says.* New York: G. P. Putnam's Sons, 1992.

Hatcher, Robert A., Shannon A. Damman and Julie Convisser. *Doctor, Am I a Virgin Again? Cases and Counsel for a Healthy Sexuality.* Atlanta, Georgia: DIVA, 1990.

Kroll, Ken and Erica L. Klein. *Enabling Romance: A Guide to Love, Sex, amd Relationships for the Disabled (And People Who Care About Them).* New York: Harmony Books/Crown Publishers, 1992.

Maksym, Diane. *Shared Feelings: A Parent's Guide to Sexuality Education for Children, Adolescents, and Adults Who Have a Mental Handicap.* North York, Ontario, Canada: The G. Allan Roeber Institute, York University, 1990.

8 Sexual Decisions in the Age of AIDS and Other Infections

Sharing sexual feelings and activities can be a wonderful experience, but it is clearly not without its risks. As we have seen in earlier chapters of this book, people get hurt in many different ways by sex, emotionally and physically. Since earliest recorded history, we know that human beings have been plagued by the diseases that are caught through sexual interaction.

Many shared sexual behaviors involve close association of various body parts, and this often provides an opportunity for body fluids of two different people to come into contact. Our body fluids naturally carry various sorts of bacteria, viruses, and other organisms. Most of the time, these organisms do not cause any particular problems. Some, however, can transmit disease from one individual to another. Some of these diseases are only minor infections that are barely noticed; others can be very serious and even deadly. Some can be cured by common medical treatments, whereas others cannot.

Passing Along Disease

It sometimes has been said that when you have sex with someone, you also are having sex with everyone else they have ever shared sex with. What that really means is that if your sexual partner has taken risks of being infected by a *sexually transmitted disease* (STD), then the risks get passed along to you as well. If the person has caught an STD, recognized its symptoms, and received medical treatment that has cured the disease, then the progress of the disease from person to person has been halted. Unfortunately, some STDs have symptoms that are rather mild or even unnoticeable for a long time. In the meantime, the germs that cause the disease may be passed along from sexual partner to sexual partner, infecting many people before anyone realizes that the disease is present.

During that period from the 1960s through the early 1980s that has been called the "sexual revolution," it was largely believed that most sexually transmitted diseases could be cured through the use of antibiotics or other treatments. Therefore, even though people knew that they risked catching a disease when they had sex, they also tended to believe that these diseases could be cured quite easily.

Eventually, however, it became clear that things were not quite that simple. It was discovered in the 1970s that a large proportion of sexually active people was infected by a viral disease called genital herpes. There was no cure, and the disease could cause outbreaks of painful sores on the sex organs over and over again. Evidence also began to mount that women who had had many different male sexual partners were more likely to get cancer of the cervix (the lower part of the uterus).

The most sobering news about sexual diseases emerged in the mid 1980s, when it became clear that a deadly disease called AIDS could be spread by sexual activity.

H.I.V. INFECTION AND AIDS

The problem was first recognized among some gay men who began to get serious infections that their bodies could not seem to fight off. It was as if their immune systems—the built-in mechanisms we have to defend our bodies against disease and cure us of diseases once we get them—had stopped working. Their bodies became more and more defenseless against germs, and eventually were overcome by various infections, resulting in death. The disease was called *acquired immunodeficiency syndrome*, or AIDS for short, because it seemed to spread from person to person and cause a weakness in the immune system.

Before long, AIDS also was recognized as a problem among groups of drug abusers who shared dirty needles for injecting drugs into their veins. Scientists began to suspect that whatever caused AIDS might be carried in body fluids such as semen and blood. After months of work, researchers in France and the United States isolated the virus that led to this fatal disease. It eventually was labeled *H.I.V.*, which stands for *human immunodeficiency virus*.

Where Did H.I.V. Come From?

Nobody can ever be sure how a disease germ gets started. Scientists now believe that H.I.V. started in Africa, and that it may have been a virus that originally caused a similar disease among a certain species of monkey. The virus may have undergone some sort of mutation that enabled it to infect humans. In any case, AIDS has become a very serious disease throughout central Africa, and has killed thousands of people. It has been transmitted mostly between men and women in these countries.

Who Can Get H.I.V.?

It is now clear that H.I.V. is transmitted when body fluids such as semen, blood, or vaginal fluids intermingle. Although H.I.V. has been found in other fluids, such as saliva and urine, it is not known if those fluids actually can transmit the disease to others.

Although the infection got its start in the United States among gay men and drug abusers who shared needles, enough people have been infected so that anyone could now be at risk. It has been estimated that between one and two million people in the United States already are infected with H.I.V., and it keeps spreading. It is just as much a risk for people who share heterosexual activities as it is for those who share homosexual behaviors. Everyone should also be very careful about coming into contact with the blood of others.

When Does AIDS Develop?

When H.I.V. infects the body, it usually does not cause any noticeable symptoms for many months. Gradually, however, it destroys the immune cells that are crucial in defending the body against disease. The body reacts to H.I.V. infection by producing substances called *antibodies* that try to fight the virus. These antibodies eventually can be detected in the body. Therefore, after six months or so, most people who have been infected by H.I.V. will have the antibodies in their bloodstream. Blood tests for H.I.V. look for the antibody. Just recently, it has been recognized that some people may take longer than six months to develop H.I.V. antibodies, and it may even be true that a new form of AIDS develops without showing any earlier signs of H.I.V. disease.

AIDS is considered to be one of the later stages of H.I.V. disease, and it is considered to be fatal. During the earlier stages of H.I.V. disease, the affected person may not feel well, and may be more prone to getting certain kinds of diseases, such as rare forms of pneumonia. As the immune system becomes further weakened, the body gets even more diseases, and eventually medical treatment cannot cure them.

The time between H.I.V. infection and the development of AIDS seems to vary a great deal among people. If an infected person gets plenty of rest, eats a highly nutritious diet, and exercises, the rate of the disease may be slowed. Some people have been infected with H.I.V. for years, and still have not developed serious disease symptoms or AIDS. In others, the infection progresses quickly. No one yet knows if some people infected with H.I.V. will be able to avoid AIDS altogether and remain free of illness.

The number of people with AIDS continues to rise alarmingly. As of late 1992, health experts were still debating the point at which H.I.V. disease should be called AIDS. Given the most widely accepted definitions, close to 400,000 people are now considered to be ill with AIDS. Medical researchers are studying a variety of medicines that may help control the disease, and vaccines that might be used to prevent its spread. However, at present there are no drugs or vaccines that can cure or prevent H.I.V. disease.

SEXUAL DECISIONS AND H.I.V./AIDS

Because of H.I.V., sex has become a very risky activity. Teenagers are among the groups in which the rate of H.I.V. infection is increasing quite rapidly. So how can we face sexual decisions in the face of the H.I.V. risks?

The quickest and easiest advice I can offer anyone is simply to avoid sharing sexual activity with other people, or in other words, to practice abstinence. That is good, realistic advice, and a choice that many young people are making in these risky times. However, in the long run, I am not sure that such advice is the most thoughtful, complete, and helpful that I might give. For one thing, statistics tell us that even in the face of the risks, a great many young people are still choosing to have sex. For another, we must ask the question of how long we abstain from sex. Even if you decide never to share sex until after you become settled in a permanent relationship such as marriage, you will still have to face the issues that anyone faces when they decide to have sex. Eventually, most people will have to make decisions about how to approach sexual activity, even with its risks. Here are the things you must consider as you make your choices about sex.

Remember That It CAN Happen to You

Only too often, people fool themselves into thinking that the bad things that happen to other people just could not happen to them. Feelings of invulnerability are particularly common among teenagers. Unfortunately, the statistics tell us all too clearly that negative consequences of sex, including getting infected with H.I.V., happen to people all the time. These are not times when you can afford to play games with your life by taking sexual decisions too lightly. It is important that you face the difficult questions head-on, and try to maintain a level of self-esteem that will enable you to make your own decisions, carefully and thoughtfully.

Do You Really Need to Share "Penetrative" Sex?

By "penetrative" sex, we mean the kind of sexual activity in which a part of one partner's body, such as the penis, a finger, or the tongue, penetrates into the other partner's body by way of the vagina, mouth, or anus. Obviously, these are the forms of sex that we have come to see as most intimate and intense. As you were reminded in Chapter 5, however, there are many forms of sexual sharing that do not require one person to penetrate another's body. Nonpenetrative sex vastly reduces the risk of body fluids mingling together, and thus reduces the chances of spreading disease. They can also be very loving and sexually satisfying ways of being together.

How Much Do You Know About Your Sexual Partner?

This issue is now more critical than ever before. It is important to have developed the levels of communication with a potential sexual partner that will enable you to know as much as possible about his or her sexual history. If your partner has had sex with others before you, then the risks for you are increased. You will need to be able to talk together about these things, and that is not always easy to do. These days, knowledge about your partner is one of the best protections you can have. Based on what you know about a sexual partner, you can make decisions about how much protection the two of you will need in your sexual interactions.

Can You Trust Your Partner?

Of course, all the talking in the world is not going to be of much value unless your partner is trustworthy. One recent research study of over 400 eighteen to twenty-five-year-olds found that 34% of the males and 10% of the females admitted to having lied about their sexual histories in order to have sex with someone. Even more disturbing, 20% of the males and 4% of the females said that they would lie about having had a negative AIDS test in order to have sex. So as much as we might want to think that we can trust others, that is not always the case. It takes time and good communication to show how much we can trust the word of others. Sometimes, there is an inner intuitive sense—the little voice inside—that will tell us whether someone is trustworthy. We need to learn to listen for all the signals that will tell us when we can trust a partner.

Can You Be Certain a Partner is Disease-free?

If your sex partner has had sex with others before you, there is at least some risk that she or he has been infected with H.I.V. or another disease germ. The only way to be absolutely sure would be to have medical tests that can determine whether a disease is present. Many couples are having such tests before going ahead with their sexual sharing. It makes good sense, and shows very real caring and consideration for one another. Keep in mind, however, that the test for H.I.V. may not show that the virus is present for up to six months or more after the person has been infected. That means that you will have to wait an appropriate amount of time after possible infection before the tests would be reliable. Most medical clinics can offer anonymous testing for H.I.V. That means you do not even have to give your name when requesting a test. Instead, you are assigned a number, and then report back after a few days for the results. Because of the seriousness of H.I.V. disease, clinics generally will not give H.I.V. test results over the telephone or by mail.

How Can You Make Sex Safer?

Remember that when you choose to share sex, the risks cannot be completely eliminated. However, you can reduce the risks significantly by the choices you make, making sex even safer. One such choice would be doing things sexually that do not involve penetration or contact with body fluids. You also can use devices that will help prevent contact with fluids. Latex rubber condoms that fit over the penis represent one of the best forms of protection. But condoms have to be used correctly (see Figure 8.1).

Condoms should be placed on the erect penis before any sexual contact has taken place. That is because fluid may come out of the penis even before ejaculation of semen. The end of the condom should be pinched so that there is no air in it, saving a space for the semen to go when it is ejaculated. The condom is then unrolled all the way down to the base of the penis and left in

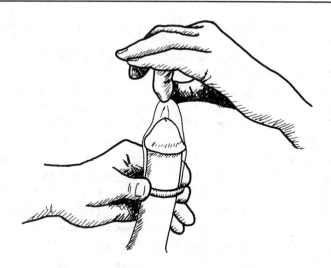

Figure 8.1 The end of a condom should be pinched while the condom is being unrolled on the erect penis. This leaves an empty space to hold the semen when it is ejaculated, reducing the chances of leakage.

place for all sexual activity. It is a good idea to check it from time to time to make sure it has not slipped at all. Never use petroleum or other oil-based lubricants with rubber condoms, because they can cause weakening and tearing of the rubber. Very soon after the male has ejaculated, he should reach down and hold the condom in place on the penis while he withdraws or moves. Because he will lose some of his erection, it is easier for the condom to slip off if he is not careful, spilling some semen.

There are other devices that can make sex safer. Some people choose to wear little rubber finger "cots" on their fingers if they are inserting them as part of sexual activity. Thin sheets of rubber often used by dentists as dental "dams" can be placed across the female vulva during oral sexual activity. Soon, a "female condom" will be available in stores (see Figure 8.2). This is a rubber pouch that is placed in the vagina, creating a safe lining that protects against infection.

These are not easy times to be growing up sexually or experimenting with sex. The risks are very real and very dangerous. However, this does not mean that sex cannot still be shared as an enjoyable part of a loving relationship. It does mean that people must care about one another sufficiently to go out of their way to protect one another, and themselves, from the unnecessary tragedy of getting a disease through sex.

How Available Should Condoms Be?

One of the controversies surrounding H.I.V. infection is the degree to which we should make condoms available to people. On one side of the debate are those who believe that making condoms available only encourages irresponsible sex. On the other side are those who feel that the more we can do to encourage safer sex by making condoms easily available, the better. They believe that condom availability is more of a health issue than it is a moral issue.

A few high schools now distribute free condoms to students upon request. Many colleges distribute condoms to students, or

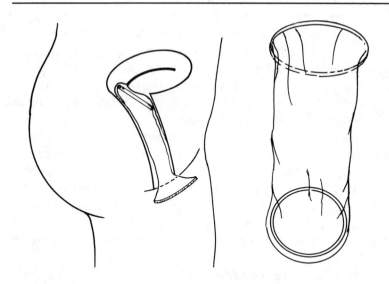

Figure 8.2 A "female condom" soon will be available for use. It is a pouch that is open at one end, and having a rubber ring at the closed end. The ring at the closed end is inserted into the back of the vagina. This product will enable a woman to make sex safer for herself and her partner.

make them available in dormitory vending machines. The debate will continue concerning the appropriateness of such decisions, but the evidence is clear that condom use vastly decreases the chances of contracting a disease from a sexual partner.

SEXUALLY TRANSMITTED DISEASES

The sexually transmitted diseases (STD), formerly called venereal diseases (VD), are transmitted by direct sexual contact. Some are considered among the most serious diseases of the world and have reached epidemic proportions during recent years. If you are sexually active, you are more likely to contract a sexually transmitted disease. Any person who is sexually active or is thinking about having sexual activity should be familiar with the symptoms, prevention, and treatment of these diseases. Most forms of STD may be treated and cured in the early stages, but putting off treatment can be dangerous.

The germs that cause sexually transmitted diseases can survive only for a few seconds in the air, so the diseases are transmitted only by direct body contact. It is not possible to catch STDs from a toilet seat, dirty dishes, or clothing. You don't catch STDs from another person because he or she is dirty. You can catch them because the other person caught them from another infected person. Like most other diseases, we really do not know where or when the sexually transmitted diseases started. They have been infecting human beings since the beginning of recorded history and probably long before. The infectious germs evolved along with other forms of life.

STDs and Their Symptoms

Any form of sexual contact in which the sex organs of one person are in direct contact with the sex organs, mouth, or anus of another can transmit the germs of most STDs, if they are present. Some of the symptoms of infection are:

Gonorrhea

Sometimes called "Clap" or "The Drip" in slang, gonorrhea is caused by bacteria that can attack the tissues lining the urethra, the cervix of women, the anus, the throat, or the eyelids.

In the penis, the symptoms usually begin to develop within a week after sexual contact with the infected person. The first sign is usually a burning and itching feeling during urination, and eventually severe pain during urination. This is usually accompanied by drainage of thick pus out of the penis. If untreated, the germs spread into the upper organs of the male reproductive system, the testes, bladder, and even the kidneys.

In the vagina, the symptoms of gonorrhea are often not as easily detected. Pain and discharge of pus may not appear until much later. In the majority of women, few symptoms are noticed until the disease has progressed into a serious infection. The most common symptoms are vaginal discharge of pus, irritation of the major and minor lips in the vulva, and frequent painful urination. Again, if the disease is untreated, the germs may spread through the uterus and into the fallopian tubes.

In the mouth and throat, gonorrhea germs do not seem to survive very long, but they may be transmitted to others while they are present. There may be a sore throat or no symptoms at all. In the anus or rectum of either sex, symptoms of gonorrhea may go unnoticed. There may be some irritation and discharge, but generally the disease goes undetected in the rectum until the germs have spread through the body. In both men and women, lack of proper medical treatment for gonorrhea can lead to dangerous complications and illness. One serious result can be sterility, the inability to have children. The germs may also enter the bloodstream, leading to arthritis and other joint infections. If a mother is infected with gonorrhea at the time she is giving birth to a child, the bacteria can infect the baby's eyes and cause blindness. As a precaution against this, medications are put in newborn babies' eyes that prevent infection.

Syphilis

This infection is caused by a germ known as a spirochete, a microscopic spiral-shaped organism. Once inside the body, the syphilis germs rapidly multiply. The disease, when untreated, has three stages:

Early syphilis. Within a month or two after contact with the infected person, a small, reddish, painless, oozing sore appears on the skin. This is called a *chancre.* When it appears on the penis it is easily noticed. In the vagina or anus, however, the chancre is usually internal and often is not discovered. The chancre may also appear on or inside the mouth or elsewhere on the body. Syphilis is particularly contagious at this stage, because the chancre is filled with the spirochetes. Even without treatment, the chancre heals in four to ten weeks. The germs have moved dangerously into the body.

Secondary syphilis may not become evident for several weeks. It is usually characterized by a rash over large portions of the body, along with a slight fever and general "rundown" feeling.

Late syphilis. If medical treatment has not been given, the syphilis germs may gradually infect any portion of the body with serious results. Untreated syphilis may eventually result in death. There are blood tests that show the presence of syphilis in its latter two stages. Rates of infection with syphilis have been rising sharply. Some states require a blood test for syphilis before issuing a marriage license to a couple. If a pregnant woman has syphilis, the germs may be transmitted to the developing fetus, causing serious malformations and birth defects.

Chlamydia

This microorganism only recently was identified as causing a widespread and potentially serious sexually transmitted disease. It is believed that there are millions of new chlamydial infections each year, and it is now the most widespread STD in the United States. Part of the danger with chlamydia is that there are often no clearly identified symptoms until serious complications have developed. It is estimated that 70% or more of infected women and 10% of infected men do not develop symptoms in the earlier stages. The early symptoms, if they do develop, are similar to those of gonorrhea. They include burning and itching in the urethra and genital area, and sometimes discharge of pus. If untreated, more painful internal infections can develop that can cause permanent damage to the reproductive organs. If a chlamydial infection exists during pregnancy, the baby may be damaged and death of the unborn baby, or occasionally of the mother, can occur. Physicians have available quick, painless, and accurate tests to diagnose this disease that is now reaching epidemic proportions.

Genital Herpes

This infection has now become one of the more common and more serious of the sexually transmitted diseases. Its name comes from the herpes virus that causes the infection, a germ very similar to the one that causes cold sores around the mouth. Usually within three weeks after sexual contact with an infected person, an area on the sex organs begins to itch or burn. Then, small, red blisters develop that become painful and ulcerated. The disease is most contagious in its blister form. In women, the blister may be internal, and therefore go unnoticed.

Like cold sores, genital herpes blisters eventually heal. However, the virus remains in the body, and there may be continuing, unpredictable flare-ups of the blisters. Because the virus is never actually eliminated from the body once contracted, there is no real "cure" for the disease. Some people never have any further outbreaks of the blisters after the initial infection. There are creams, which appear to reduce discomfort, that may be applied to the blisters.

There are two potential dangers for women with herpes infections. Medical researchers suspect that the virus may be one cause of cervical (in the cervix of the uterus) cancer. In addition, the virus can infect babies during the birth process, leading to serious disease or death of the infant. For this reason, caesarean delivery (see Chapter 9) is often recommended for pregnant women who are known to have an active herpes infection.

Genital warts, or Condyloma

Characterized by wart growths in or on the sex organs, condyloma also are caused by a virus. They are uncomfortable, and often painful. Medical treatment is important and usually involves surgical removal of the warts.

Hepatitis B

This is a viral liver infection often spread by sexual contact. There are many other forms of hepatitis that are not sexually transmitted, but hepatitis B is most typically spread through sex. It is especially common among homosexual males who participate in anal intercourse (see Chapter Five). The infection is characterized by fever, chills, nausea and a generally sick feeling that may persist for weeks. Although liver infections can sometimes be fatal, hepatitis B usually clears up on its own eventually. A new vaccine to prevent the disease is currently being tested, and may soon be available as a preventive measure.

Pubic lice

Also called "crabs," these are tiny blood-sucking insects that become parasitic on the body. They most commonly infect the pubic hair area, causing troublesome itching. Other body hair regions may become infected, however. Although they are usually transmitted by direct body contact, this is one STD that may also be picked up through contact with contaminated bedding, clothes, towels, or toilet seats. Ordinary soap will not destroy pubic lice, but there are several prescribed medicated creams that will take care of them rapidly. Sheets, clothing, and other potentially contaminated materials must also be washed to prevent re-infection.

Non Specific Urethritis (N.S.U.)

This refers to any infection of the urethra, and it may be caused by a variety of bacteria and yeasts that are spread through sexual contact. N.S.U. usually causes itching and burning that may be particularly evident during or after urination. The symptoms may be quite mild or severe, and such infections can be transmitted during sexual activity. One of the common causes of urethritis is chlamydia. Only a competent medical person will be capable of distinguishing between gonorrhea, chlamydia, and N.S.U.

Other diseases associated with sex organs

There are three other sexually transmitted diseases that are less common in North America, but that can be very dangerous. They are chancroid, lymphogranuloma venereum (LGV), and granuloma inguinale. There are also many types of infections and inflammations that may affect the sex organs, although they are not all associated with sexual contact. Any discomfort, sores, warts, or inflammations of the genitals should be discussed with a physician or STD clinic staff member regardless of their cause.

Treatment of STDs

Gonorrhea, syphilis, and chlamydia are easily treated by a medical clinician, and may be cured by injection or oral doses of penicillin or other antibiotic. Taking penicillin pills alone will not cure gonorrhea or syphilis, and may be dangerous without a doctor's supervision. Pubic lice and most forms of urethritis also respond well to medical treatment. Because they are caused by viruses, herpes, venereal warts, and hepatitis B are not curable by any medicine, but their uncomfortable symptoms may be relieved by appropriate treatment. Anyone who suspects the presence of a sexually transmitted disease should seek medical attention immediately! Simple tests can show whether or not the diseases are present, and—if so—appropriate treatment can be given. Many locations have clinics to treat STD, sometimes without charge. Public health agencies, telephone crisis centers, and counselors can often provide addresses of clinics and other health services.

Informing partners that you may have infected them with an STD or that you may have contracted STD from them is also a part of responsible sex. It may be difficult and embarrassing, but you owe it to them so they may seek treatment and prevent further spread of the disease. Some health agencies will ask for your contacts, but rarely are all of these people followed up. If you find out you have any sexually transmitted disease, informing endangered contacts is your responsibility.

There is an organization that provides a national, toll-free telephone hot line to offer information about sexually transmitted diseases. If you have any questions, or want to know the location of the nearest STD treatment clinic, the free telephone number of the National STD Hotline is 1-800-227-8922 (8 A.M. to 11 P.M. EST, weekdays). No one will ask your name, and calls are completely confidential.

Avoiding STDs

Sexually transmitted diseases can be prevented. The fact of the matter is that you must be extremely cautious about choosing a sexual partner, and the ways in which you participate in sex. Unless you can be absolutely certain that your partner has never had sex with anyone else, or has not shared hypodermic needles with others, you cannot be absolutely certain that the individual is not a carrier of disease. For specific suggestions on making sex safer, see pages 158–160 earlier in this chapter.

EXAMINING YOUR ATTITUDES ABOUT H.I.V. AND STD

There are several important value questions that you may want to ask yourself. Where would you stand on the following issues?

You have been dating a person for several months, but have not been sexually active together. Your partner suggests to you that maybe it is time in the relationship to begin considering having sex together. Your partner has told you before that he (she) has had sex with two other people in the past, but you do not know any other details. In making your decision about whether to become sexually involved with this person, what would you need and want to know?

If you really wanted to have sex with someone, would you ever consider lying about whether you have had sex before? If you have had sex, do you feel that you can be absolutely certain you did not contract any disease? If you are not certain, what are you going to do about it?

What would you recommend to a friend who confides to you that she (he) recently had sexual intercourse, but discovered afterward that the condom had broken?

Consider a situation in which you might be thinking about having sex with someone you deeply care about. You know that before proceeding into sex, it will be important to talk more about the other person's past sexual experiences. You know that this communication will be somewhat awkward. What are the things that make communicating the most difficult? What reactions would you fear most from the other individual? How might you begin the conversation?

Examining Your Risks

Consider the following statements, and decide whether you agree or disagree with each one. Rate each statement with a number, taken from this rating scale:

5 = I strongly agree with this statement
4 = I agree with this statement
3 = I am uncertain about this statement
2 = I disagree with this statement
1 = I strongly disagree with this statement

Rating:

___ 1. It is difficult to prevent sexually transmitted diseases.

___ 2. If I were sexually active, I would be uncomfortable doing the things before and after sex that would help prevent STD.

___ 3. It would be embarrassing to discuss STDs with a person I might consider having sex with.

___ 4. Abstaining from sex is not a good way to prevent the spread of STDs.

___ 5. The chance of getting an STD would not stop me from having sex.

___ 6. I do not intend to limit (or have not limited) my sexual activity to just one partner.

___ 7. If I were sexually active, I think it would be insulting to a sexual partner to suggest that we use a condom.

___ 8. If I had an STD, I would not want to tell public health officials who the person was that I got it from.

___ 9. I would be reluctant to talk about sexually transmitted diseases with someone close to me.

___ 10. I would dislike having to follow the medical steps necessary for treating an STD.

_____ Your Total Score

Scores on this evaluation could range from 10 to 50, assuming that you rated yourself for every statement. Although it is not a completely reliable "test," the higher your score is, the higher the risk that your behavior could spread a sexually transmitted disease.

Go back and consider how you rated each statement. Do your ratings reflect some degree of difficulty in dealing realistically with the threat of STDs in sexual interactions? How might you want to work at changing your attitudes so that you would be even less likely to spread STDs?

Topics for Further Study

Information about H.I.V., AIDS, and the sexually transmitted diseases is always being updated. Here are some questions that you might want to answer through some research on your own:

1. How many people in this country are currently believed to have been infected with H.I.V.?
2. What is the most common STD among teenagers and college students?
3. How close are we to having a vaccine that could prevent H.I.V. infection and AIDS?
4. Who is on the National AIDS Commission, and what is this group currently recommending?
5. Why is it that "skin" condoms are not recommended for the prevention of H.I.V. infection, but latex rubber condoms are?

For Further Reading

Baker, Ronald, Jeffrey Moulton and John C. Tighe. *Early Care for HIV Disease.* San Francisco, California: Impact AIDS, 1992.

Blake, J., *Risky Times: How to be AIDS-smart and Stay Healthy.* New York: Workman Publishing Co., 1990.

Douglas, Paul H. and Laura Pinsky. *The Essential AIDS Fact Book.* New York: Pocket Books, 1989.

Holmes. K. K., et. al. *Sexually Transmitted Diseases.* New York: McGraw-Hill, 1990.

White, Ryan and Ann Marie Cunningham. *Ryan White: My Own Story.* (A personal account of a young man with AIDS.) New York: Dial Books, 1991.

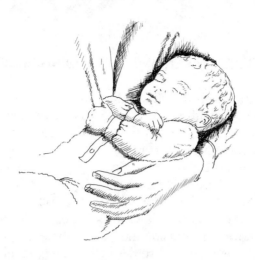

9 A Parent: To Be or Not To Be

This chapter is about having children and being a parent, and not having children. Having a baby is indeed a miraculous process, although there is no special trick to it. Most women, during their childbearing years, and most men have the capability of creating a pregnancy. With the effective methods of birth control now available, all men and women also have the capability of preventing a pregnancy. Parenthood is a more complicated issue. Being a good parent doesn't just happen; it requires certain qualities and it means working on the development of certain attitudes.

The decision to have a child must be approached with caution and careful thought. Child-raising requires much attention, time, and money. In fact, the average cost of raising a child to the age of eighteen is now about $100,000. Children also need parents who can provide love, security, and good models for reaching responsible adulthood. Parents are the ones who give personalities and values to the next generation, and that is a big responsibility not only to the children, but to society.

FAMILIES, PARENTING, AND HAVING BABIES

It was traditionally believed that children were best raised within a marriage, with a mother who was the homemaker and a father who held a job and earned money to support the family. Many families simply no longer fit this traditional image of what a family "should" be. Although having two parents in the home can make it easier to share all of the responsibilities of raising children, single parents also do a fine job of parenting. The structure of the family has been changing in other ways. For example, the majority of mothers now work outside the home. Some gay and lesbian individuals or couples also are raising children, either from previous heterosexual marriages or through adoption.

Regardless of the structure of any particular family, children seem to do best when they are raised with a sense of security, stability, warmth, and love. Single parents, and other nontraditional families, are able to provide healthy environments in which children may grow and develop.

What Makes a "Good Parent"?

There is a great deal of disagreement on the "best" ways to raise children. Like everything else, the qualities each individual parent displays depend on all of the other aspects of his or her personality. Yet, there seem to be some fundamental characteristics essential to effective parenthood:

1. *A desire to have children*
   It helps to want children and to like them. When children are unexpected, unwanted, or considered a nuisance, they are bound to create more tension.

2. *Security and stability*
   Children tend to grow up healthy and happy when they are given a sense of basic security and stability. This doesn't mean plenty of money, but instead it means a feeling of strength and consistency from their parents. This not only

helps them trust the world around them, but helps them to trust themselves.

3. *Warmth, trust, and respect*

   Children depend on their parents for many things, including food and shelter. Most psychologists agree that they also depend on their parents—especially during their early years—for human warmth and caring. Children need to feel loved and worth loving. Parents also must try to trust their children and respect them as individuals.

4. *Sharing and communicating*

   Parents are people, too, and children need to share in their feelings, ideas, and values. Likewise, children need to be able to let parents know what is going on inside. It's up to parents to set the climate where two-way communication can happen. Good listening on the part of the parent is an important part of that climate.

5. *Setting rules*

   Children and teenagers need to know the limits that they have. Parents have the difficult responsibility of establishing fair rules, setting good examples for their children, and being fair about enforcing the rules.

There are plenty of other qualities that could be mentioned. One thing is certain: being a good parent is one of the most difficult, time-consuming jobs that people can ever have. Parenthood should be a decision reached with great care. In the next section, we'll take a look at how a new human being is created.

Conception—The Beginning

Several times in earlier chapters, we have talked about our sexual feelings and their importance to our lives. One of the important functions of our sex organs is *reproduction*—producing more of our species. Be sure you understand the anatomy of the reproductive systems described in Chapter 2 before you try to understand how reproduction occurs.

Remember that the male's testes produce millions of microscopic, swimming *sperm*. The sperm are suspended in the *semen,* which the male ejaculates when he experiences orgasm. The female's ovaries produce *eggs* or *ova,* usually one about every month. After the egg or *ovum* has broken through the wall of the ovary at ovulation, it moves along through the fallopian tube for two or three days.

During sexual intercourse, the semen may be ejaculated from the erect penis of the male into the vagina of the female. Gradually, the semen seeps through the opening of the cervix and into the uterus. The millions of sperm in the semen swim further into the female reproductive organs. Sperm can probably live from three to five days within the female reproductive system. Eventually, they reach the fallopian tubes. If an ovum is present in one of the tubes, one of the sperm may penetrate the outer wall of the ovum and enter it. This is called *fertilization* or *conception,* and a pregnancy has begun. As soon as the sperm has fertilized the ovum, a change occurs in the ovum's outer layers so that no more sperm may enter.

It is sometimes possible for pregnancy to occur even if actual sexual intercourse has not occurred. If, during sex play, the male ejaculates semen near the opening of the vagina, it is possible for some of the semen to get into the vagina. The sperm in the semen may fertilize the ovum. Remember—although the more sperm present, the more likelihood of fertilization, it only takes *one* sperm to fertilize an ovum. Some couples make the mistake of thinking that if the male withdraws his penis before ejaculating, pregnancy cannot result. Actually, the clear fluid from Cowper's glands, which comes out of the penis during sexual arousal, may carry some sperm and therefore create the possibility of pregnancy.

Implantation in the Uterus

Soon after the ovum has been fertilized, it begins the process of cell division. It divides first to form two cells; then both of these divide, forming four cells. The cells continue to divide until a spherical mass of cells has formed. The entire mass of cells is no bigger than the tiny ovum was before fertilization.

All of this cell division takes place as the fertilized ovum continues to move down the fallopian tubes and into the uterus. After seven or eight days, the mass of cells becomes attached to the inner wall of the uterus and produces special enzymes that help it to dissolve some of the uterine lining. Gradually, it buries itself within the lining. This is called *implantation*. (See Figure 9.1)

The cells of the developing *embryo* absorb food from the surrounding tissues of the uterus and begin to grow. Cell division continues until three layers gradually form the developing baby's

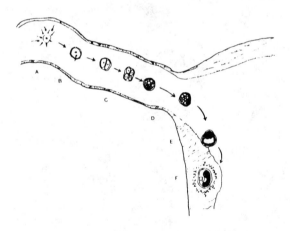

Figure 9.1 Fertilization and implantation. The ovum is surrounded by sperm (A) and is eventually fertilized by one sperm (B). It then begins to divide (C). For several days, cell division continues (D) as the developing embryo moves into the uterus. Within 7 or 8 days, the mass of cells has made contact with the uterine wall (E), and gradually becomes implanted there (F).

organs. One layer becomes the nervous system, skin, sense organs, and mouth. Another layer becomes the respiratory and digestive systems. The third layer develops into muscles, bones, blood vessels, and sex organs.

While the embryo is growing and developing, special membranes form around it. One is a tough sac around the embryo, filled with fluid. This is the *amnion* or "bag of waters." The amnion provides a moist cushion that protects the embryo suspended in it.

Another structure that forms along the uterine lining as the embryo grows is the *placenta*. The embryo eventually is con-

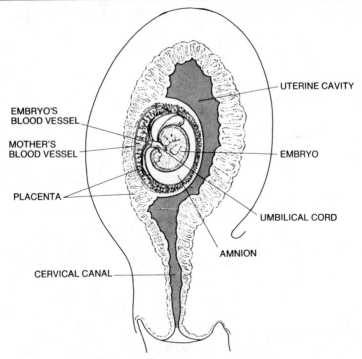

Figure 9.2 Blood vessels from the embryo travel through the umbilical cord into the placenta, where they come very near the blood vessels of the mother. Although the two blood systems do not mix, they are close enough so that materials may be exchanged between them.

nected to the placenta by its *umbilical cord*. These are important structures for bringing nourishment to the developing embryo.

Blood vessels from the embryo connect to special vessels leading through the umbilical cord into the placenta and back again. They come very close to blood vessels from the mother's body which extend into the placenta. The blood of the embryo and its mother come very close together, but they do not mix (Figure 9.2). However, they are close enough so that oxygen and nutrients enter the embryo's bloodstream. Also, waste products from the embryo leave its blood and pass into the mother's body. Her kidneys and lungs then get rid of the waste products. The lungs, digestive system, and kidneys of the embryo do not need to function fully until after birth. The placenta gets larger as the developing baby grows until at the time of birth, the placenta is a large roundish mass of tissue, several inches in diameter and more than an inch thick. The umbilical cord grows to a length of about twenty inches.

Infertility and Reproductive Technology

Not all women and men are physically able to create a pregnancy. This is called *infertility*. Some men do not produce sperm, or do not produce them in sufficient numbers to have a good chance of fertilizing an egg. Some women do not produce eggs, or they have abnormalities of the reproductive organs that do not allow fertilization or implantation to take place. For couples who desire children, infertility can cause a great deal of psychological stress and tension for the relationship. However, there are several forms of medical treatment that can help infertile couples increase their chances of getting pregnant.

The new reproductive technologies have been creating hope for couples who have been having difficulty getting pregnant. Although many of the newer techniques still have a relatively low success rate and may be quite expensive, many couples have been turning to clinics that use these techniques.

One of the oldest techniques is *artificial insemination*, in which a male's sperm are placed in a woman's vagina by a clinician. If the woman's partner cannot produce enough sperm, a physician can obtain semen from another male donor, and use it to artificially inseminate the woman. This results in pregnancy 60% to 75% of the time. There are also techniques for separating sperm cells out of the semen of a man who has a low sperm count. This concentrates the sperm. Some clinics then actually insert the concentrated sperm directly into the woman's fallopian tubes. This combination of approaches makes it more likely for pregnancy to occur.

Some infertile women have blockages within the fallopian tubes that make it impossible for the sperm and egg to meet. One of the newer reproductive technologies has been having limited success in helping such women. It is *in vitro fertilization*, or *IVF*. Eggs are removed directly from the woman's ovaries, and fertilized in the laboratory with her partner's sperm. Then the fertilized egg is placed back in the woman's uterus, in hopes that it will implant itself and develop into an embryo. Babies born as a result of this technique have sometimes been called "test-tube babies," because conception takes place in a laboratory.

One of the more controversial techniques has been the use of a "surrogate" or substitute mother to carry the pregnancy and give birth to a child. The surrogate mother may become impregnated by artificial insemination, using sperm from the other woman's male partner. Or the fertilized egg may be donated by the other couple by means of IVF. The surrogate agrees to accept a sum of money to then give birth to the child and turn it over to the couple who wants to have a baby. This has led to some court battles with surrogate mothers who have changed their minds and decided to keep the babies themselves. Some states have passed laws prohibiting the use of surrogates for pregnancy. This is a good example of how reproductive technologies carry with them complicated ethical issues that have not been resolved completely.

Boy or Girl and How Many?

It is the *chromosomes,* present in the cells of the embryo, that determine almost all of the physical characteristics of the new human being: its eventual size and bone structure; the color of its skin, eyes, and hair; its sex; and everything else. The sperm and ovum contain 23 chromosomes each. When fertilization occurs, these sets of chromosomes combine to form 46. As cell division proceeds and the embryo grows, each new cell gets a full set of 46 chromosomes.

Since the embryo gets half of its chromosomes from the mother and half from the father, its characteristics will be a blend of the traits carried by those chromosomes. Which traits show themselves and which do not are explained by the science of *genetics,* not covered in this book.

The sex of a child—whether it will be a boy or girl—is determined at the moment of fertilization. The ovum carries one chromosome that helps determine the sex of the embryo; it is called the *X chromosome.* Sperm also carry one sex-determining chromosome, but they may carry either an *X chromosome* or a *Y chromosome.* If a sperm that fertilizes the ovum carries an X chromosome, it combines with the ovum's X, and forms a female (XX). If the sperm carries a Y chromosome, the XY combination

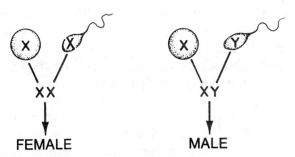

Figure 9.3 Sex chromosomes in the sperm and ovum determine the sex of the child at the time of fertilization.

forms a male (see Figure 9.3). Although the infant's sex is determined at fertilization, the actual sex organs do not become visible
until late in the third month of development.

Multiple births—twins, triplets, and so on—also are formed
very early in development. *Fraternal twins* are the result of the
ovaries producing two separate eggs or ova, both of which are
fertilized by separate sperm. These twins may be the same or
opposite sex and look no more alike than any other children in the
family might be expected to look. *Identical twins,* however, result
from a single ovum being fertilized by a single sperm. When the
fertilized ovum divides for the first time, the new cells separate
completely, each developing into an embryo. Since their cells
carry identical chromosomes, their physical traits are also identical (Figure 9.4). Triplets may be formed by fertilization of three
separate ova, or two ova, one splitting at the first cell division.
Other multiple births involve similar combinations.

Fetal Development

From fertilization to birth, nine months are required for
development of the fetus to the extent that it can survive outside of
the uterus. A baby that is born before the full nine months are
completed is said to be *premature.* The earlier it is born, the less
chance of survival. Babies born during the seventh month now
have a good chance of living. Most babies born during the eighth
or ninth month survive. Fewer babies born before the seventh
month live, although larger medical centers have neonatal intensive care units that can greatly increase their chances of survival.

After the embryo has been growing and developing for two
months, it is usually called a *fetus*. Tremendous changes occur in
the fetus as it begins to take on the characteristics of a human
being. By the time it is born, the fetus weighs *6 billion times* more
than when it was a fertilized ovum. There are few identifiable
human characteristics until the third month of pregnancy. By then,
the fetus is two to three inches in length, and fingers, toes, and
facial features are visible. As Figure 9.5 shows, the fetus gradually

looks more and more like a human being as growth and development continue.

Signs and Limitations of Pregnancy

When a woman is pregnant, the first possible indications include not experiencing menstruation, nausea and vomiting in the morning, fatigue, changes in the size and fullness of the breasts, and more frequent urination. Of course, these symptoms may have other causes too, or may not appear during pregnancy.

There are several tests that physicians can administer to determine whether or not a woman is pregnant. Home pregnancy test kits are also widely available in drug stores, without prescription. Some of these tests are more accurate than others. If the test is positive, indicating pregnancy, a physician or family planning clinic should be consulted. Often, the test will be repeated there to confirm the pregnancy.

The clinician will also do an internal examination, looking for changes in the cervix and size of the uterus. A mucus plug appears in the opening of the cervix that apparently prevents

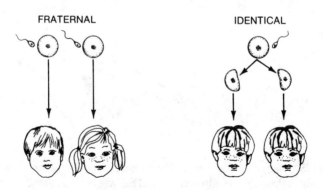

Figure 9.4 Twins are either fraternal, formed from two separate ova fertilized by two separate sperm; or identical, formed from one ovum fertilized by one sperm, then dividing.

germs and other material from entering the uterus and endangering the embryo. Signs that are detected later in pregnancy are the movements of the fetus and hearing the fetal heartbeat with a stethoscope. The fetus may also be seen in a special sound wave picture called a sonogram.

A healthy pregnant woman is encouraged to pursue her normal activities. Unless the physician recommends it there is no reason to limit travel, exercise, or sexual activity during pregnancy. In the last four to six weeks before birth, sexual intercourse may become difficult because of the woman's large abdomen, but different positions for intercourse sometimes are successful. Some couples use other forms of sexual gratification—such as mutual masturbation—during the final weeks of pregnancy.

The Birth Process

After the nine months of development, the baby is born. Childbirth is a process about which there is a great deal of misunderstanding and unnecessary fear. For pregnant women who are

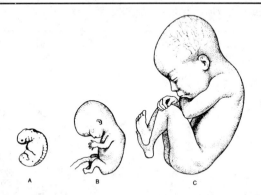

Figure 9.5   Many changes occur as the fetus develops. (A) Embryo at 4 weeks, about $1/12$ inch in length; (B) Fetus at $8^{1}/_{2}$ weeks, 1 inch long, weighing $1/15$ ounce; (C) The fetus at 16 weeks, about 8 inches long and weighing about 6 ounces. By this time, the movements of the fetus may be felt and its heartbeat detected with a stethoscope.

helped to understand what will happen when their child is born, the birth process can become a cooperative effort among herself, trained medical professionals, and her partner. It need not be a frightening and painful mystery.

There are three signs that can indicate that the birth process is starting. The most common signal is the beginning of powerful muscle contractions called *labor* in the uterus. At first, the contractions occur every 15 to 20 minutes, and last about 30 seconds each. Gradually, the labor contractions become stronger and occur more frequently, until they are coming every 3 to 4 minutes. Labor usually lasts between 8 and 20 hours. Each uterine contraction moves the fetus farther down toward the vagina. The opening in the cervix gradually widens to a diameter of about 4 inches.

The second sign that may appear early in the birth process is the expelling of the mucus plug from the opening to the uterus. Another sign may be the breaking of the amnion, or bag of waters, so that the fluid that protects the baby flows out of the vagina. Sometimes, the amnion does not break until much later in labor.

When the opening of the cervix is completely open, the fetus slowly moves into the vagina, now called the *birth canal*. The vagina is capable of stretching a great deal to accommodate the emerging baby. The fetus is usually in a head-first position (see Figure 9.6). Occasionally a fetus is in a backward (breech) or sideways position and may require special attention from the physician delivering it, usually an *obstetrician*. An hour or two is normally required for the fetus to move through the birth canal.

If delivery of the baby occurs in the hospital, the mother usually lies on a delivery table, with her knees bent and thighs wide apart. As the baby's head emerges through the opening to the vagina, the mother's tissues must stretch a great deal. During the latter stages of birth, it is important for the mother to help push the baby out by contracting her abdominal muscles. Once the infant's head has fully emerged, its body turns to the right or left.

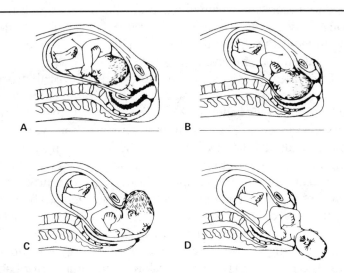

Figure 9.6 The Birth Process. (A) The fetus inside the uterus as the birth process begins. (B) The cervix has widened and the baby moves through the birth canal. (C) The baby's head becomes visible in the vaginal opening. (D) The baby's body turns and one shoulder emerges. (From *Human Sexuality* by James Leslie McCary, copyright 1978 by Litton Educational Publishing, Inc. Reprinted by permission of D. Van Nostrand Company.)

The clinician then helps guide the shoulders out. The remainder of the baby's body emerges easily and rapidly (see Figure 9.6).

The umbilical cord is still attached to the baby after birth. The obstetrician ties the cord in two places and cuts it close to the infant's body. Whatever is left will eventually fall off, leaving the navel or "belly button." About 15 minutes following the baby's birth, the placenta—left inside the uterus—along with the remaining portion of umbilical cord, are also expelled from the uterus through the vagina. This process is sometimes called the *afterbirth*.

Giving birth to a baby is hard work and involves some pain at various stages of labor and delivery. Many women now participate in classes to prepare for childbirth. The father of the baby, or someone else close to the mother, takes the same classes to learn how to be a "coach" during labor and delivery. They learn relaxation and breathing techniques to relieve some discomfort of labor contractions, and also practice the pushing movements necessary to delivery of the baby. Most hospitals now allow the father, or other coach, to be present for the entire birth process.

If there is some problem with the normal birth process described above, the obstetrician or surgeon may have to perform a special operation called a *caesarean section*. In this procedure, a cut is made in the abdomen and through the uterus, and the baby is removed from the uterus through the cut. The term caesarean section originated from the legend that Julius Caesar was brought into the world in this manner.

Once the child has been born, the difficult process of parenting must begin. In fact, there is increasing research evidence to indicate that loving contact between the parents and the newborn baby is extremely important even in the first hour or two after it is born. There may be a process of *bonding* that occurs between parents and their children during that period. The cycle of human life continues, with the process of reproduction as its principal source of inertia.

CHOOSING NOT TO BECOME A PARENT

It is apparent that many couples have children for the wrong reasons. Every couple must think carefully about their reasons for having children, and be cautious that they have not been trapped into some of these wrong reasons:

1. *Because couples are "supposed" to have children*
   Many married couples get pressure from their parents and

others to hurry up and have children, even before they have had sufficient time to adjust to one another. Studies show that it is often wise to wait until later in the marriage before the extra pressures and problems of children are created. In fact, there are some couples who never want to have children, and they are able to lead happy, fulfilled lives together.

2. *To "strengthen" the relationship*

Some couples who are having trouble with their relationships decide that having a child may patch things up. Actually, pregnancy and giving birth may bring the couples closer together temporarily, but if their deeper problems are not worked out, they are bound to re-appear later on. Then, the child may only add to the difficulties and be affected by them. Remember — babies aren't marriage counselors.

3. *Because babies and children are so cute and fun to have around*

They may be just that much of the time, but they also take a lot of work, energy, and money. And as they get older, they may have their moments of being rebellious and uncooperative. They sometimes get sick. Anyone who looks only at the positive aspects of kids is probably being unrealistic.

So, there may be plenty of good reasons for a couple to delay having children until *they* are ready, or not to have children at all. Some couples decide to adopt children rather than have their own, since there are many youngsters who need good homes.

Family Planning

Most professionals agree that successful marriage and successful parenthood are helped along by careful planning of the family. That means deciding when to start having children, how many to have, and how often to have them, in light of the family's financial situation and the readiness of the parents.

Several research studies indicate that children and their parents tend to be happier and better adjusted when there are fewer, well-spaced children. The myths about the spoiled only child are not supported by facts either. Studies show that only children often are physically and mentally healthier, and achieve greater success in later life than children who have brothers and sisters.

Successful family planning will depend on the use of methods of *birth control,* or *contraception* while the couple is choosing not to have a child. Responsible sex between a woman and a man must include the use of birth control methods whenever there is the risk of an unintended pregnancy. It should also be noted that pregnancy *can* occur whenever sexual intercourse occurs, even with contraceptive protection. Contraception greatly reduces the chances of pregnancy, but cannot eliminate them. Some methods of contraception are more effective and reliable than others. Any partners who feel ready to share sexual intercourse also should be ready to discuss birth control and to decide together which method(s) they wish to use. The following sections of this chapter provide more information on the various methods.

Types of Birth Control

One method of birth control is *abstinence*—not participating in sexual intercourse. Some couples make this choice, especially unmarried couples. They may substitute other forms of sexual activity for intercourse. As noted in earlier chapters of this book, abstinence works very well, unless people change their minds and decide to share sex.

For couples who choose to have sexual intercourse, yet wish to delay children until later in their lives, there are several ways of preventing fertilization. One of the most widely used methods, though not particularly reliable, is *withdrawal of the penis* from the vagina before ejaculation. Through the years, several methods have been developed to *prevent the sperm from reaching the ovum.* These include use of the *condom, the diaphragm,* and *chemicals that kill sperm* (spermicides).

Through changing hormone levels in the female's body, the *ovum may be prevented from leaving the ovary.* The *birth control pill,* and several other hormonal methods, work this way. Another device is the *intrauterine device (IUD),* although the manner in which it prevents pregnancy is poorly understood. Some couples attempt to have sexual intercourse during times in the woman's menstrual cycle when the ovum is not likely to be in the fallopian tubes. This is called *natural family planning/fertility awareness.* Each of these methods will be discussed in more detail.

Withdrawal of the penis

Withdrawal from the vagina before ejaculation is obviously a very unreliable method of birth control, although some couples manage to use it successfully. One danger is that sperm may be present in the Cowper's gland fluid, which comes out of the penis *before* ejaculation. A further disadvantage is that it requires careful control and attention by the male partner. He must "stay tuned in" to himself so that he knows when ejaculation is about to occur, and then pull out in time. Some men find this difficult or impossible, regardless of their good intentions. Many couples feel that the need for such control does not permit relaxed, enjoyable sex. Statistics show a high failure rate for this method, so it is one of the more unreliable methods for preventing pregnancy. It is however, better than using no method of birth control at all.

The condom

Placed on the penis before intercourse begins and worn during intercourse, the condom's function is to collect the semen when ejaculation occurs, so that it does not enter the vagina. Most condoms are made of very thin rubber, which does not interfere with the sensations of sex, although more expensive condoms made of animal membranes are also available (sometimes called "skins").

Condoms are available in drugstores and now even in many other stores, and no doctor's prescription is needed. The most reliable condoms are individually wrapped. They are rolled into a ring, which is then unrolled out onto the erect penis. Some condoms have a small space built-in at the end for collection of the semen. If such a space is not built-in, a small amount of space should be left at the tip of the condom for the semen. While the

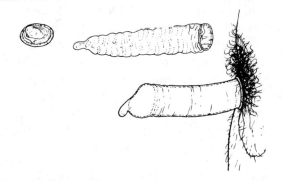

Figure 9.7 The condom: rolled; unrolled; unrolled on the erect penis, with space at the tip to collect semen.

condom is being unrolled onto the penis, the space at its end should be pinched so that it will not even contain air (see Figure 9.7).

The two main dangers when using the condom are breakage and slippage. It is possible for the condom to break during intercourse or to slip off the penis, especially after ejaculation when the penis begins to lose its erection. Occasional checking of the condom during intercourse is wise, and when the penis is withdrawn, the *condom should be held on* with the fingers so that it does not slip off in the vagina. Rubber condoms become weakened easily, and should *not* be stored in a warm place such as a wallet or glove compartment in a car. Some condoms are lubricated to make entry into the vagina easier. Petroleum jellies such as Vaseline, or other oil-based lubricants will dissolve the rubber, causing breakage of a condom.

The effectiveness of condoms is improved when used with a sperm-killing chemical. A further advantage of the latex rubber condom is that it offers good protection against the spread of sexually transmitted diseases and H.I.V. Skin condoms apparently do not provide the same degree of protection against viruses.

The female condom

Discussed in Chapter 8 (page 160), the female condom is a pouch that can be inserted into the vagina, lining it as a protection from pregnancy and disease. At this writing, the female condom has not yet been approved for marketing to the general public. When it does become available, preliminary tests indicate that it should be about as effective as the male condom for preventing conception and the spread of disease germs. It is also the only method of birth control that also protects against disease for which the woman may take complete responsibility.

Chemicals that kill sperm: spermicides

These come in the form of creams, jellies, foams, or suppositories. They should be inserted into the vagina, as directed on the package, *immediately before each intercourse.* Their failure rate when used alone is high so they are *better used along with the condom or diaphragm.* They prevent fertilization by helping to block the entrance to the uterus so that semen does not enter it and by killing the sperm. These chemicals are also available without prescription in drug stores and supermarkets. A relatively new method of contraception is the *birth control sponge,* available without prescription. They are placed over the cervix at the back of the vagina, and contain a spermicidal chemical.

The diaphragm

A cup of thin rubber stretched over a ring, the diaphragm is inserted with the fingers into the back of the vagina and placed over the cervix of the uterus (see Figure 9.8). A sperm-killing cream or jelly is placed on the diaphragm to make it more effective. A diaphragm must be fitted for a woman by a trained medical person. It is inserted into the vagina within six hours before intercourse, and then should not be removed until at least six hours after intercourse, although it may be left in for up to twenty-four hours. Used with spermicidal jelly, the diaphragm is very effective.

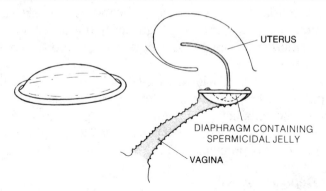

Figure 9.8 The diaphragm, showing a side view of its internal position when placed over the cervix.

The pill

This is a form of oral contraception, because the pills are taken by mouth. Birth control pills contain hormones that prevent ovulation, the releasing of an ovum by the ovaries. If the ovum is not present in the female's fallopian tubes, fertilization cannot occur. There are several different types of birth control pills, and a medical clinician must weigh factors of age and health in deciding whether it is a suitable method of birth control and which type should be prescribed. Then, the pills must be taken faithfully every day, about the same time of day, as directed. If pills are skipped, the risk of pregnancy increases.

There has been some controversy over the use of birth control pills because there is a possibility of some unpleasant side effects. Research has shown that women over age thirty-five and those who smoke should not use the pill because of the increased risk of side effects. However, the consensus seems to be that when prescribed and used under the supervision of a physician, the risks of birth control pills are lower than the risks accompanying pregnancy. Myths about the pill's dangers have developed over the years, but research tends to show that it is a relatively safe form of contraception. It even has been shown to help prevent certain types of ovarian and uterine cancer. The more carelessly it is used, of course, the more chance of pregnancy or unwanted side effects. If any side effects appear, the physician should be consulted immediately.

Some girls have made the mistake of "borrowing" birth control pills from their mother or a friend. This is a dangerous practice because the pills have not been properly prescribed for them. Some have mistakenly believed that *one pill* will do the job, often with the result of pregnancy.

Depo-Provera
This is a hormone that may be given by injection. A single dose of this contraceptive will prevent ovulation for about three months. Birth control injections just recently have been approved for use in the United States.

Norplant implants
These consist of six slender rubber capsules, each about the size of a matchstick. The capsules contain a contraceptive chemical that prevents ovulation. They are surgically implanted under the skin of a woman's upper arm, and slowly release the chemical into her bloodstream for up to five years. They represent a handy form of birth control for someone who wants long-term protection from pregnancy. Norplant implants tend to have many of the same side effects as birth control pills, and these effects tend to be most troublesome during the first year after they are implanted.

The intrauterine device (IUD)
Available from around 1960, IUDs have been made in a variety of shapes, usually out of flexible plastic or metal (see Figure 9.9). The IUD has been associated with higher risks of internal infections, and for a time became much less available. Its popularity is slowly increasing again, but most clinicians are reluctant to prescribe it for younger women. The IUD is inserted by a family planning clinician directly into the uterus. A fine thread

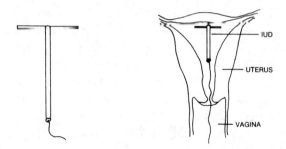

Figure 9.9 An IUD, shown in place inside the uterus. An IUD must be inserted by a clinician.

extends out into the vagina so that the woman or her partner can check occasionally to make sure the IUD is still in place.

There is disagreement as to how the IUD actually works. The most widely accepted idea is that the device somehow interferes with the implantation of an embryo in the wall of the uterus. Some women experience some discomfort after an IUD has been inserted, and there is a chance of the uterus expelling the device. When pregnancy is desired, the IUD must be removed by a qualified professional.

Natural family planning/fertility awareness

This involves careful attention to the woman's menstrual cycle so that sexual intercourse does not take place when the ovum is present and may be fertilized. It is a "natural" method of birth control considered acceptable to the Roman Catholic Church. Typically, women experience ovulation 14 to 16 days before their next menstrual period is to begin. At that time, the ovum is present in the fallopian tube for about 2 days and could be fertilized. So for a few days before, during, and after that time, sexual intercourse could lead to pregnancy and is avoided, or other forms of birth control are used. The difficult part of this method is determining when ovulation takes place. Again, this is best figured out with the aid of a family planning specialist, who will help the woman keep careful records of her menstrual cycle over a period of several months. This part of the method has been called the *rhythm method,* and is not considered very reliable when used alone. However, natural family planning uses two additional methods of determining when ovulation occurs. The *basal body temperature method,* for example, uses measures of body temperature to help pinpoint when ovulation takes place. The *cervical mucus method* requires regular checking of the consistency of mucus around the cervix, at the back of the vagina. This consistency changes around the time of ovulation.

There are a number of potential problems with this method. For those girls and women whose menstrual cycles are irregular and vary in length from month to month, predicting ovulation may be difficult. Natural family planning/fertility awareness is most likely to be successful when used by couples living together in a stable relationship where their life cycles are reasonably predictable and the commitment to cooperating together on the method is strong. Because it is a complicated method, it is best taught by a qualified professional.

Sterilization

A procedure by which a man or woman is made incapable of reproducing is called sterilization. More and more people—especially after having a certain number of children—are choosing to be sterilized. Women are usually sterilized by a cutting and/or tying of the fallopian tubes. This is called *tubal ligation.* Physicians are also experimenting with plugs that can be inserted into the fallopian tubes, and then removed when pregnancy is desired. Other more complicated surgery that involves removal of the ovaries or uterus also leads to sterilization, though it would not be done solely for that purpose. The most common method for male sterilization is a simple procedure called a *vasectomy,* in which the vas deferens—the tube that leads sperm upward from the testes—is cut and tied. Although these sterilization procedures are sometimes reversible, they should be considered relatively permanent. Therefore, if there is any possibility of an individual desiring children at a later time, they should not be employed.

Other birth control methods

New forms of birth control are being developed through research, and more reliable, convenient techniques may soon be available. The Federal Food and Drug Administration approved a *vaginal contraceptive film,* a papery substance with a spermicidal chemical, placed at the back of the vagina prior to intercourse.

There has been a good deal of discussion about birth control pills for men that would cause temporary sterility. Such a pill would either prevent production of sperm in the testes or inactivate the sperm in some way. Researchers report that the pill for males is still a fair distance away, and marketing studies indicate that men will be reluctant to take it.

Birth Control that Doesn't Work

In the past, many myths have developed about methods of birth control. Except for the techniques described earlier, these methods can be expected to have little, if any, effectiveness. One old and ineffective method is *douching,* washing out the vagina after intercourse. A variety of douches have been suggested, including various kinds of soft drinks such as Coca-Cola. These do not wash the sperm out and prevent pregnancy. Most physicians agree that douching usually serves no useful function unless prescribed for a vaginal infection, and may actually harm the linings of the vagina. The vaginal sprays sold in stores are for perfuming purposes only and *not* for birth control.

Another myth holds that if the woman does not reach orgasm, she cannot become pregnant. Ovulation has nothing to do with orgasm, so there is just as much chance for pregnancy with or without orgasm. Having intercourse during the woman's menstrual period, when the menstrual flow is present, also offers no guarantee that pregnancy will not occur.

It is also not true that pregnancy cannot occur the first time a girl experiences intercourse. Pregnancy can indeed result from the first intercourse.

Choosing the "Best" Method of Birth Control

Any individuals or couples who expect to have sexual intercourse should carefully consider the various methods of birth control and decide which seem most suitable and available to them. Birth control is not the responsibility of *just* the man or *just* the woman, but of *both partners*. A sexual encounter in which both partners assume that the other has provided for birth control, without any discussion, is an irresponsible encounter. If one partner lies about being protected by birth control, irresponsible exploitation is occurring. It should be kept in mind, too, that more than one method of birth control may be used. The more methods employed, the greater the protection.

Young people often ask me what form of birth control would be the most effective for them. Actually, most contraceptive methods are quite effective when used *correctly* and *consistently*. The important thing is to learn as much as possible about the positive and negative features of each method, and then to choose the method that seems to suit one's needs and sexual life-style best. Most types of birth control have potential risks and dangers, and all of them have their inconvenient features. Some groups discourage the use of "non-natural" forms of contraception that introduce hormones or chemicals into the woman's body, whereas medical groups counter that the protective benefits of these methods outweigh the risks. It is essential for any couple to choose a method with which both partners feel comfortable, that both understand, that is affordable, and that they both can commit themselves to using *every* time they share sex. It is also important to remember that couples may use more than one form of birth control during the course of their relationship.

The laws of different states vary concerning the age at which a person may obtain birth control materials. Your local Planned

Parenthood or Family Planning agency can provide you with appropriate information concerning your state. These organizations are often best equipped to give complete education about the various contraceptive methods, and then help in the decision making process. They can also often provide counseling help for people attempting to make decisions about sex or unwanted pregnancy. For more information on your local agencies, look in your telephone directory or write to one of the organizations listed in Appendix II.

OPTIONS FOR UNINTENDED PREGNANCY

Some young people make the mistake of thinking "it couldn't happen to me." They fool themselves into thinking that "just once won't matter," or believe the silly myths about pregnancy. The fact remains that *any time sexual intercourse takes place, there is some risk of pregnancy.* Even the most reliable methods of birth control can fail, resulting in an unintended pregnancy. So, any couple choosing to share sex should think and talk about what they might do should an unintended pregnancy occur.

This can be a very difficult problem, with many feelings and decisions to be faced. Talking things over with a good counselor may be important. Briefly, there are three main options available. One is to keep the baby. This choice necessitates decisions about whether or not the couple will marry, who will actually raise the child, whether or not the parents' education can continue, and so on. A second option is to have the baby and offer it for adoption. Most adoption agencies have long lists of couples hoping to be able to adopt babies.

Adoption

Up until the early 1970s, most young women who had unintended pregnancies placed their babies for adoption. The situation now is quite different, and only about 5% of mothers now make a baby available for adoption. Adoption agencies find it difficult to provide newborn babies for the many childless couples who would like to be able to adopt one. This is largely due to negative attitudes that have developed about adoption. Many young people have negative reactions toward "giving up a child" for adoption.

Although there are certainly some emotional consequences of allowing one's child to be adopted, it often turns out to be a very desirable option for an unintended pregnancy. In some cases, adopted children continue to have contact with one or both of their biological parents. Other times, information about the biological parents is not made available unless there is some sort of parental medical information that is required for the child's well-being.

Abortion

This is the third option available in cases of unintended pregnancy. *Abortion* refers to the explusion of a growing embryo or fetus from the uterus, thus ending the pregnancy before the baby is born. This sometimes occurs as the result of natural causes, and is then called a *spontaneous abortion* or *miscarriage*.

There are also methods by which a physician can induce abortion. In years past, when induced abortion was illegal except for very special cases, many pregnant girls and women sought illegal abortions from untrained persons. These dangerous procedures often led to injury, disease, or even death. As the result of new state laws and a 1973 Supreme Court decision in *Roe vs. Wade,* safe and legal abortions by qualified physicians may be obtained in many areas. There are many individuals and some religious and political groups who object to abortion on moral grounds, insisting that it is tantamount to killing another human being. This is sometimes called the Pro-Life or Right to Life point of view. An opposite point of view is that a fetus is part of a woman's body and that the woman should have the right to decide whether or not she wishes to give birth to the child. This usually is called the Pro-

Choice stance. Most professionals agree that effective contraception is certainly better than having to resort to an abortion, but abortion is an option that many pregnant women still wish to choose. It should not be considered a form of birth control, because the pregnancy is actually terminated.

Abortions may be induced several ways by a physician, although this is best done during the first trimester, or first three months of pregnancy. Most methods involve the insertion of some instrument into the uterus, which evacuates the uterine contents. In later weeks of pregnancy, it may be necessary to inject a saline solution into the uterus causing eventual expulsion of the fetus from the uterus. When done by a properly trained physician, an abortion—especially during the early weeks—can be done safely, quickly, without much discomfort, and at a cost of around $300. Some clinics or family planning agencies offer abortions at minimal cost or even free of charge.

There has been controversy over the possible psychological consequences of having an abortion. More research needs to be done to fully understand what these consequences might be. Obviously, with the publicity about abortion from both sides of the debate, it is an issue about which people tend to have strong feelings. A woman who is considering having an abortion should weigh her values and feelings very carefully in making the decision, and consider the values of those around her. So far, there have not been legal precedents that have given the father any particular rights in making the decision. However, fathers often have reactions and feelings relating to abortion as well.

There does not seem to be much evidence to support the claim that many women suffer serious emotional reactions following an abortion. In fact, most seem to get through any reactions without undue problems. Support from friends and family, and professional counseling, can help those women who have an especially difficult time with their feelings.

Many clinics and physicians have become more reluctant to offer abortions to girls who have not reached the legal age of majority, unless they have signed consent from the girl's parent. In some states, there are now laws that make obtaining an abortion even more difficult. Over the next few years, the abortion issue will continue to be fought in the courts and through the political process.

A Final Note on Parenthood

Teenage mothers and fathers often face serious problems. They may be treated unfairly by parents, friends, schools, and society. They often feel guilty and afraid as they face the confusion of deciding what to do. Some communities have special programs and counseling available for teenage mothers and fathers. Planned Parenthood and other Family Planning agencies may be able to provide further information.

It must also be kept in mind that the world is facing the crunch of overpopulation. In underdeveloped countries, this problem leads to disease, misery, and starvation, but overpopulation is very much a problem in the more developed, industrialized countries of the world too. Every new child in developed countries uses massive amounts of food and resources and contributes vast amounts of garbage to our pollution problems.

The earth's population grows at an astounding rate. Its first billion living inhabitants were not acquired until 1830. By 1950, the earth's population had reached 2.5 billion and by 1990, the population of the world had reached 5.3 billion people. Population experts and other scientists agree that this growing number of people could have disastrous effects for all of us, as we get low on food and sources of energy and high on pollution.

This represents simply another reason why sex—and its role in reproduction—carries with it important responsibilities. Our sexual feelings can provide us with the utmost pleasure and fulfillment. Yet, seeking the gratification of sex must mean paying attention to our responsibilities—to oursevles, our sexual partners, and our world.

FOR FURTHER EXPLORATION

Parenthood

On a separate paper, make a list of the qualities you feel are important for good parents to have. Take into consideration such things as the kind of relationship they have as a couple and with their children; financial security; personal characteristics; abilities for communication; age; level of maturity; and emotional stability.

Now go back and carefully consider the list you made. How would you rate yourself in each of the qualities you have listed? It might help to rate each quality with a number from the following scale:

1.	2.	3.	4.
I have a long way to go	I'm getting closer all the time, but have plenty of time	Before long, I'll be there	I'm ready now on this score

On a separate sheet of paper, make two columns with the following headings:

(1)	(2)
Areas where my parents excelled, and where I want to be the same with my children:	Areas where my parents could have done better, and where I would like to be different with my children:

Now, choosing from the following list, place items in the column where they fit best for you. Also, feel free to add your own items:

Showing warmth and love	Teaching about sex
Trying to understand	Showing and sharing inner feelings
Demonstrating trust	
Setting good examples	Communication
Knowing when to compromise	Not judging too quickly
Making fair rules	Allowing children's friends in the home
Being fair in enforcing rules	
Giving the right amount of advice	Giving a good allowance
	Knowing when to show approval
Knowing when *not* to belittle	
Providing security and stability	Accepting differing values

Further research on conception, birth, and babies

Using the books listed at the end of this chapter or references you can find in a library, try to find more information on the following subjects:

- What happens when a sperm fertilizes an ovum?
- What are the stages of growth that a fetus goes through during each week of its development?
- What is "natural childbirth" and "Lamaze childbirth"?
- How are identical twins formed, and how often do they occur?
- Fertility drugs are sometimes used to help a woman become pregnant. How do these drugs work and why do they sometimes lead to multiple births—twins, triplets, or more?
- What are all of the functions of the amnion, placenta, and umbilical cord?
- Why is an isolette often used when a baby is born prematurely? What does the isolette do?

If you have never had much contact with babies during their first few months of life, try to visit an infant day-care center or to spend some time with a new mother. Try to get a better idea of the amount of care required by a baby. After you have had some time to think about your observations, make two lists:
(1) The things you like *most* about babies and taking care of them;

(2) The things that appeal to you *least* about babies and caring for them.

Birth Control

What information would you want to give these friends of yours in the following situations? Remember, there are no pat "right" or "wrong" ways to respond. Do what *you* think is best:

A 16-year-old boy who is a friend of yours tells you that he and his girlfriend have had sexual intercourse several times. You inquire about the method of birth control they are using, and he tells you that they are just trying to be careful to avoid intercourse during the middle of the month.

A 15-year-old girl you know has just discovered that she is pregnant, but she has not yet talked about her problem with anyone. You are the first person she has told. She tells you that she wants to have an abortion but does not know how or where to obtain one.

You are talking about birth control with a friend of your own sex and age. The friend insists that it is the girl's responsibility to use birth control because she is the one who gets pregnant. Your friend also believes that the particular method of birth control used is unimportant, saying "they all work if you use them right."

Do you think you would like to have children some day? If so, how many would you like to have? What are your reasons for thinking that this is your "ideal" family? Is the family larger or smaller than the family in which you were raised? What have you learned from the size of your family?

For Further Reading

Bullough, Vern and Bonnie Bullough. *Contraception: A Guide to Birth Control Methods*. Buffalo, New York: Prometheus Books, 1990.

Everett, Jane and Walter Glanze. *The Condom Book: The Essential Guide for Men and Women*. New York: Signet Books, 1987.

Feldman, S. *Making Up Your Mind About Motherhood*. New York: Bantam Books, 1985.

Hatcher, Robert A., et. al. *Contraceptive Technology*. (16th ed.) New York: Irvington Press, 1993.

Lindsay, J. W. *Pregnant Too Soon: Adoption is an Option*. Buena Park, California: Morning Glory Press, 1988.

10 Preventing and Coping with Sexual Harassment and Abuse

While walking through the school bus to find her seat, Jennifer is embarrassed by two boys who yell, "Look at those boobs!" One of them reaches out and grabs at her thigh, but she pulls away and sits down. Some of the other kids on the bus are looking at her and laughing.

Jason doesn't like sports much, and doesn't see himself as particularly athletic. While playing basketball in physical education class, he attempted to pass the ball to another player, but it fell short and bounced out of bounds. Somebody yelled, "Sissy pass. You throw like a girl." Another boy said, "What are you, a fag?"

Anna had been overjoyed to find a summer job at a fast food restaurant near her home. One of her friends who had worked at the restaurant before told her to watch out for the manager who worked the same shift, a man in his early twenties. Anna was not overly concerned, because she knew she would be around other people whenever she worked. After she had been there for a few days, the manager called her and a teenage boy aside and told them a sexual joke that Anna found embarrassing. The manager and the boy both laughed, and so Anna did as well. Over a period of several weeks, the manager continued to tell her and other employees suggestive jokes and stories that made her uncomfortable. She put up with them, and even pretended to find them funny, because she was afraid if she told the manager to stop, it could jeopardize her chances at getting the job again in the future.

On his first camping trip with several other boys, Tim shared a tent with Ken. After everyone had settled down for the night, Ken turned on his flashlight and said to Tim, "Let's jerk off." Tim was embarrassed and said that he didn't want to, but Ken persisted. He told Tim that it was all part of the fun when camping. Tim found himself curious, but still felt confused and scared. Ken reached over and pulled down Tim's sleeping bag, again insisting that Tim join him.

After a school dance, Julie's boyfriend invited her over to his house to watch TV. When they arrived, she realized that the boy's parents were not home, and he told her that they would be gone for two more hours. Before long, the two were kissing on the couch, and touching each other's body. Julie's boyfriend said that he was getting very turned on, and she admitted that she was too. Finally, she decided that she wanted to stop because she felt things were getting out of control. The boy urged her to continue, saying, "You can't leave me like this." She was feeling uncertain of how firm to be, and reminded him that she didn't want to go too far. He said he wouldn't pressure her, and they resumed their fooling around.

When the boy began reaching under her skirt to pull down her underpants, she started to push him away. He kept pressing her down on the couch, and eventually had sexual intercourse with her, even though Julie kept telling him she did not want to.

Bob was tall for age fifteen, and prided himself on his muscular body that he was developing by lifting weights. During a family reunion at his grandmother's house, Bob's aunt—a woman in her late twenties—called Bob into an upstairs bedroom. She started kissing him, and eventually slipped her hand down the front of his pants and fondled his sex organs. Bob pulled away, feeling embarrassed and startled. He had enjoyed the sensations, but somehow felt uncomfortable that his father's sister was being so intimate with him. She was laughing as he left the room, and Bob felt as though he did not want to hurt her or his father by telling anyone about the experience.

Walking through the parking lot at a shopping mall, Maria saw a car driving toward her. The man in the car was rolling down his window, and seemed to be motioning for her to come nearer. He asked her for directions to another mall. As she began to explain how he could find the stores, he asked her to come closer because he couldn't hear her. Then she realized that the man had pulled down his pants and was showing her his penis.

Michael had run away from home because of several serious disagreements with his parents. For several days, he lived on city streets, eating and sleeping wherever he could. An older boy befriended him, and helped him find food and shelter. Michael was becoming increasingly depressed by his situation, and began to realize that living without any source of money was going to be very difficult. His older friend suggested that he try getting money by selling himself for sex.

One evening while she was babysitting her younger brother at home, Yvonne's telephone rang. When she answered, there were a few moments of silence followed by a male voice whispering. At first, she couldn't make out what he was saying, and kept asking him to speak up. Then she realized that the male on the phone was making obscene and sexually suggestive comments. She tried asking who the caller was, but when he persisted with the obscenities, she hung up. Frightened by the call, she called her mother at work and asked her to come home.

All of the incidents that these young people experienced have one thing in common. They are all forms of sexual harassment or abuse. They represent exploitative sex-related behaviors that are unwelcome, hurtful, or upsetting, forced upon people against their will, or imposed on an individual who is considered by law to be too young to make a choice about being involved.

Another aspect of these forms of sexual exploitation is that the victims often end up feeling guilty about what happened, or as if they somehow were responsible for the actions of the other person. This chapter deals with several different forms of sexual exploitation, and offers suggestions for preventing them. However, prevention is not always possible. The chapter also suggests ways in which you can take appropriate action if you have been subjected to some form of exploitation.

SEXUAL HARASSMENT

Sexual harassment refers to any unwanted sexual advances, suggestiveness, or coercion. These actions become clearly harassing when they are repeated even after someone has been asked that they be stopped. It is particularly common in school and work settings, where people spend much time together. Sexual harassment has been given a great deal of attention by the media in recent years, and statistics show that more than half of girls and women report having been subjected to sexual harassment at some point in their lives. Males can be sexually harassed as well, either by other males or by females, but this happens much less frequently.

Some examples of potentially sexually harassing behaviors would be:

> Making comments about a person's clothing, appearance, or body.
> Sexual comments, jokes, or stories.
> Asking about information concerning one's sex life.
> Whistling, catcalls, kissing sounds.
> Repeated pressure for dates or sexual activities.
> Staring at a person, looking her/him up and down.
> Following someone around, or blocking their path.
> Standing too close or brushing up against the person.
> Hugging, patting, or stroking.
> Making obscene or sexually suggestive gestures.
> Displaying sexual pictures, cartoons, novelty toys.

The important thing to keep in mind is that whether any particular behavior is sexually harassing will depend on how welcome it is, and if it is repeated even after the individual has been asked to stop. You might not be offended or harassed by the behavior from someone you know well. The same behavior from another person may make you uncomfortable, and you will want to make it clear that you do not appreciate it.

Sometimes, sexual harassment takes place where there is some form of "power" imbalance between the people. For example, adults or teenagers usually are seen as having a more powerful social position than children. Professional people, such as teachers, counselors, and medical personnel, also are viewed as being in somewhat powerful positions over the students or patients with whom they work. When a power imbalance exists, sexual harassment becomes particularly complicated. The younger person, or the one who feels in any way less powerful, may feel very reluctant to object to the actions that seem offensive or hurtful. The individual being victimized may end up feeling helpless, even more powerless to prevent or control sexual advances that are being made.

There are now laws that prohibit sexual harassment, and many schools and workplaces have specific policies regulating against such behavior. However, rules about inappropriate conduct between peers are often much less clear, and school personnel sometimes do not take complaints of harassment as seriously as they should.

How Do You Know It's Harassment?

Because of increased awareness of sexual harassment, some teenagers are no longer putting up with behavior that once would have been tolerated. For example, some girls are making it clear that they no longer consider sexual comments, jokes, or touching to be acceptable. Boys have been expressing some confusion over the whole thing, because they have not thought of their own behaviors as being offensive or inappropriate. Sometimes, they even see their remarks or behaviors as being complimentary rather than offensive.

One of the problems here is that there can be a very fine line between acceptability and harassment, and part of that judgment may lie with the person toward whom the behavior is directed. One individual may be flattered by comments that another person would find embarrassing.

There are some general guidelines that can help you avoid doing something that another person may find sexually harassing or inappropriate. Consider them carefully:

1. *Think before you act or speak.*
   Because we now know that many people are offended by

remarks or actions that are sexual in nature, it is always a good idea to think carefully about how your own behaviors or words might be perceived by others. For example, if you think someone in your school is particularly attractive or sexy, you can offer a compliment without making the person unnecessarily uncomfortable. "You look really nice today" is a much better way of expressing your appreciation for their looks than something like, "I wish I could get my hands on those."

2. *Be considerate of the reactions of others.*

Everybody makes mistakes, and there is always a possibility that you will say or do something that you thought was perfectly innocent, but the other person will be offended by it. If you do, apologize and be more considerate in the future. If you notice that someone has been embarrassed or hurt by something you have said or done, then don't repeat it.

3. *Don't leer and don't touch.*

Some people are uncomfortable when they feel themselves being "undressed" by another's eyes. Leering stares can be embarrassing, and therefore can be harassing. So before you leer at someone, it is best to make sure they appreciate it. The problem here is that you may not be able to be certain how another person feels about the attention you are paying to them unless they tell you. One very clear rule, however, is that you should not touch another person in other than a casual way unless they have let you know that it is all right with them. One young man I know was surprised to learn that the girl whose hair he had been enjoying stroking found his actions to be too intimate. He had been assuming that it was all right with her, and she had failed to give him clear signals that she found his touching inappropriate.

What to Do if You Feel Sexually Harassed

That brings us to the other side of responsibility in issues of sexual harassment. If you feel you are being in any way harassed, it is crucial that you let the harasser know, so that he or she may have a chance to stop. This is not always easy, because you may even have mixed feelings about the actions yourself. On the one hand, you may feel somewhat pleased that someone is paying attention to you and finding you attractive. At the same time, you may feel uncomfortable with the behavior. This is the point at which you have a responsibility to let the person know that you are uncomfortable. Mixed signals may only lead the individual to believe that you are enjoying and encouraging the behavior. So the rules for dealing with sexual harassment are:

1. *Be clear about your own needs.*
   Be careful about letting your own fear or guilt get in the way. If you do not appreciate someone else's words or behaviors, be firm in your resolve to put an end to the situation.
2. *Find a way to let the other person know your feelings.*
   This may be as simple as pulling away, or saying something like, "Please don't do (say) that again." Support your words with your actions too. You can be firm without seeming to be unnecessarily nasty. But if you're too polite or smiling while you are expressing yourself, you may be sending mixed signals. If face-to-face confrontation feels uncomfortable to you, then try writing a note or letter to the individual, making it clear what behavior you do not appreciate and that you want it to stop. Explain how the behavior makes you feel, and explain what kind of relationship you would rather have (or not have) with the person. Keep a dated copy of the note, so if you have to go further with preventive action, you will have proof that you have tried to end the harassment.
3. *Get support from friends, family, or others you trust.*
   It may help to be able to talk out your confusion and concern with others, and get their support through a difficult situation. This may help you to put the incident into clearer perspective, and make decisions about how you want to

proceed. You may also want to find out if others have ever been harassed by the same person. If so, you may be able to support one another in making sure the harasser is stopped.

4. *Find out about sexual harassment policies that might apply and what authorities might be able to help you.*

   If you are being harassed in school or at work, there may well be policies specifically designed to prohibit such conduct. You will want to know what policies are in place for your protection, and what individuals are available to enforce these policies. Even if your school does not have a defined sexual harassment policy, the administrators and teachers in the school have a responsibility to make sure your environment is not sexually uncomfortable for you. Bring problems to their attention, and ask for their assistance. Involve a parent or other adult advocate if you feel you need help with dealing with authorities.

5. *If you believe you are being sexually harassed by a teacher or other adult authority, take action immediately.*

   These are upsetting and confusing situations. Again, it may seem flattering to be getting the attentions of an adult, but it is also a very real problem. Adults have the responsibility of not placing young people in sexually uncomfortable spots. Seek the help of another adult whom you trust, and be certain to take action as soon as possible. If you allow the sexual harassment to continue, things may only get worse.

   Sexual harassment is a confusing issue, and there are many different points of view about it. If your school does not already have a policy against sexual harassment, you might want to become involved in encouraging school officials to develop one. The bottom line is that no one should have to feel sexually offended or intruded upon by others. Every school and workplace should be a place where one does not have to fear sexual harassment.

SEXUAL ABUSE

The term *sexual abuse* usually refers to sexual activity between a teenager or adult and someone younger. Sexual abuse may take the form of the older individual exposing sex organs or pornographic materials to the younger person, or actually involving them in physical sexual activity.

One form of sexual abuse occurs when an adult persuades a child into some sort of sexual encounter. Some adults are particularly sexually attracted to youngsters and will attempt to take advantage of them. There are laws that prohibit these activities, and society and the courts often deal severely with offenders. It is true that children in some cases may seem not to object to the sexual advances of an adult, but courts usually place the burden of responsibility on the adult. Young people can be confused about sexual feelings, making them even more vulnerable to such adult exploitation. It is important for children to learn that their bodies are their own, and that grown-ups do not have the right to intrude on their private body parts.

In recent years, there has been a great deal of publicity about sexual abuse. This may be one of the reasons for increased reporting of such incidents. Studies of adults have found that close to 33% of women, and 16% of men, report having been sexually abused as children.

There can be negative effects on victims of sexual abuse, especially if force is used or if the abuse continues over a period of time. It may make young people feel powerless and vulnerable. This is not to say that it always leads to serious personal problems or sexual difficulties. However, if you feel that you have been sexually abused, you have nothing to feel guilty about. Instead, you should take actions to make sure the abuse does not continue, and to talk over your feelings and reactions with a counselor who can help you make sense of them.

Sometimes sexual abuse of children by adults takes place between members of the same family. The term *incest* refers to sexual activity between persons who are closely related (brother-sister; father-daughter; mother-son). Incest often involves heterosexual behavior, but sexual activity may also occur between close relatives of the same sex. There are laws that prohibit incest, and our society is unaccepting of such behavior. Most professionals believe that incest is more common than the statistics would suggest. Some young people suffer much anxiety and guilt about sexual activity with a relative, or sexual feelings for a family member, and may benefit from talking with a good counselor about their feelings. There are always people available who will be willing to help.

It is scary to think about reporting any kind of sexual abuse, whether it is within the family or not. Authorities usually are required to take action against a sexual abuser once he or she has been reported. This may include arresting abusers and making sure they receive appropriate psychological treatment. Social service and police agencies deal with abuse cases all the time, and are usually well trained in how to manage them. Again, if you feel you have been sexually victimized, it is important that you report it to a trusted adult. Sometimes, adults would rather not face such uncomfortable situations, and may instead accuse young people of lying or trying to get attention. If you get that sort of reaction, seek help from someone else. You may also want to call a local or state social service agency, which will respond by sending an investigator to find out more about the abuse and take appropriate action.

Remember: no one, including a member of your family, has the right to look at your sex organs, touch your body in sexual ways, make you look at their body or watch their sexual activities, or have sex with you, unless you are completely willing, and unless you are considered legally old enough to make such a decision. If you are being coerced into the activity by threats of harm to yourself or others if you tell anyone about being abused, you have the right to seek help from someone who will be able to protect you. Take action.

RAPE

The term rape refers to a person being forced to participate in sexual activities without her or his willingness and consent, often through physical force or threats. The victim is most often a woman, forced into sexual activity by a man. This is a crime that girls and women find particularly frightening, because it represents the most violent form of sexual exploitation. There are courses and books that help to inform women about ways of preventing rape. Women's groups are encouraging rape victims to report the crime to authorities and to follow through to prosecution. In the past, laws made prosecution of rapists difficult. More recently, however, laws have made conviction of rapists more likely, and police officials and lawyers have become more aware of their own prejudices in dealing with these cases.

People may be raped by strangers or by people they know, acquaintances. Acquaintance rape—being forced to have sex by someone known to you—is the most common form of rape. Up to 25% of college-age women report having been forced into sexual activities during dating. The statistics on males being forced into sex, either by another male or by a female, are less clear. In fact, there is a myth that males are never forced into sex, because they are always willing partners. Professionals actually estimate that about 10% of sexual assault victims are male. Unfortunately, boys and men are more likely to be so embarrassed by being sexually assaulted that they do not report the incident or take any action against the offender.

Our society's confusing attitudes about sex probably play a role in acquaintance rape. For one thing, there is a myth created by many movies and stories that women appear to resist sex while wanting men to go ahead and press for it. Everyone has seen film scenes where the woman pushes and fights against a man, and then suddenly begins to kiss and caress him willingly. Boys often have bought into the myth that it is their job to keep pressuring girls until they finally give in. Unfortunately, this can mean that males don't accept a "No" from females.

As with other forms of sexual exploitation, victims of rape often wonder if they were not somehow at fault for what happened. They may blame themselves for the clothes they wore or the ways in which they behaved, assuming that they caused the rape to happen. The fact of the matter is that you *never* lose your right to say no to any form of sex. If someone forces you into a sexual encounter, you are a victim of sexual assault. It was not by your choice, and it was not your fault.

Guidelines for Girls in Preventing Acquaintance Rape

It is important to state again that rape is not always preventable. Most women who are raped can look back and realize how trapped they were by their situation. It is important that if you are sexually assaulted, you not blame yourself. Instead, you will want to take appropriate action to deal with your feelings and to protect yourself in the future. These guidelines may help you think through the ways in which you can help reduce the chances of acquaintance rape. You should not assume that every boy would be willing to rape, for in fact the majority of boys and men would never want to force a female into some sexual act. However, it makes good sense to protect yourself in any way that you can.

1. *Watch for warning signals that a boy may be prone to disrespectfulness or violence toward girls.*
   Experts have identified some signals that may mean a male does not have positive attitudes toward the opposite sex. For example, if he does not listen well or seems to ignore what you say, it may mean he does not respect your wishes and opinions. If he seems to want to be more physically involved than you do, and does not adequately recognize your discomfort, or if he disregards your wishes in other matters, then it may mean he does not consider you important to his deci-

sion-making. Males who are overly jealous and possessive may try to make you feel guilty about resisting their sexual advances. If you notice other signs that a boy thinks of women as having a responsibility to serve men in various ways, or if he has a tendency to drink heavily and become abusive, then you will want to weigh very carefully whether this is an individual who is safe to be around.

2. *Remember your right to set limits.*
   When you get sexually aroused, you may feel somewhat "swept away" by your emotions. That is one of the reasons you may want to set clear limits for yourself and your partner even before you get physically involved. But even if you already have become physically involved, you always have the right to stop and talk through what is happening and where you are going to go with it.

3. *Be clear and assertive about your needs and wishes.*
   Polite approaches sometimes can be misinterpreted or ignored. Say "No" and mean it. Sending mixed signals only will confuse the situation, and may lead to further problems with the male.

4. *Keep in mind that nonverbal actions send a message too.*
   The way you dress and behave around boys will send a message to them, and you want to be cautious that your message is not being misinterpreted. Dressing in a "sexy" manner will get you attention and admiration, but it may also send a signal that you want to have sex. I am not meaning to suggest that girls must feel guilty about certain kinds of attire, or that it will be their fault if they are sexually assaulted. However, we never should lose sight of the nonverbal signals that we may be sending to others. Ask yourself if those potential signals are accurately representing you as a person.

5. *Watch for clues from males, and trust your intuition.*
   Pay attention to the ways in which a boy is acting around you, and the kinds of things he is saying to you. You will want to pay attention to your own inner sense of what is going on,

your intuition. If you feel uncomfortable, pressured, or confused, it may be that you will need to be more cautious.

6. *Avoid situations and behaviors that may increase the danger of being sexually assaulted.*

Being alone with a boy in an isolated area may not be the best choice if you cannot completely trust him. Getting sexually aroused together may complicate the situation even more. Use of alcohol or other drugs is often a part of the problem in acquaintance rape, because they can cloud one's judgment. So be careful where you go and how much you compromise your ability to make decisions and communicate clearly.

Guidelines for Boys to Prevent Acquaintance Rape

If you read the material for girls immediately preceding this section, it may seem to you that I have made all boys out to be sex-crazed rapists. I know that is not the case, and instead that most males want very much to be responsible about their sexual decisions and actions. However, we cannot lose sight of the fact that boys must take responsibility for their behaviors too, and to be cautious that they do not end up having sex with someone who really did not want to participate. Here are some suggestions for minimizing that risk:

1. *Know your sexual desires and limits, and be willing to communicate them clearly.*

It is not always easy to back away from being sexually turned on, but it may sometimes be necessary. Know where you need to be careful and take responsibility for your decisions. Remember that it is all right not to "score."

2. *When a girl says "No," accept it and always assume she means it.*

Don't try to be a mind reader, and don't make the assumption she just wants you to keep going. When she says "No," it is time to stop what you are doing and talk. Many males make the mistake of thinking that a girl doesn't really mean to stop.

Don't make that mistake, because you will have to pay the consequences of your actions as well.

3. *If you get turned down for sex, you do not have to see it as a personal rejection.*

   If a girl says "No," you do not have to see it as a rejection of you. She is simply expressing the fact that she does not want to participate in sex with you at that time. It is your responsibility to respect that decision. Sexual desires may be very strong, but you never lose the responsibility of controlling your behaviors.

4. *Don't assume that a "sexy" dresser or talker wants to have sex.*

   People dress and speak the way they do for many different reasons. Sometimes, they know their choice of clothes, mannerisms, or speech create attention. Most everyone wants to be seen as attractive and even sexy. That does *not* mean they are anxious to have sex. Be careful not to misread the signals.

5. *Even if a girl has willingly shared sex previously, it is not fair to assume that she will want to have sex another time.*

   Only too often, a boy will assume that once a girl has taken the step to have sex, either with him or with another boy, she will continue being willing. Permission for sexual contact during prior times together should not be taken to mean that permission will exist for any future contact. And once a girl has had sex with you, or anyone else, it does not mean that she has lost the right to make her own decision with each and every sexual opportunity.

6. *Avoid situations and behaviors that may reduce your abilities to make careful and responsible decisions about sex.*

   This may mean that you will want to be careful about the situations you get yourself into, and how turned on you allow yourself to get. It is always more difficult to make clear-headed decisions when you are intensely aroused sexually. However, this never can excuse behavior that is offensive or undesired by another person. It is also a good idea not to use alcohol or drugs in conjunction with sexually arousing situations, because they can cloud good judgment as well.

Everyone shares the responsibility of preventing acquaintance rape, and that requires respect for oneself and others, use of effective communication skills, and thinking ahead. The lives of both girls and boys can be deeply affected by acquaintance rape and its aftermath. Plan now to avoid these negative consequences.

Stranger Rape

To be sexually assaulted by a stranger is highly traumatic. This is not as common a form of rape as acquaintance rape, but it is a very upsetting form. Most girls and women fear the possibility of being raped. The dangers of being subjected to assault lead experts to warn females that they should be cautious about being alone in areas or at times when abduction by a rapist would be possible.

What to Do if You Are Raped

Experts give different kinds of advice on how to act if you are sexually assaulted. Some recommend screaming or yelling for help, and there are classes that teach girls and women skills to defend themselves physically. Others claim that if you fight a rapist who is capable of overpowering you, you are only increasing the chances of being more seriously injured, or even killed. Most experts agree that if the rape seems inevitable, you should not take any action that might incite more physical violence on the part of the rapist.

When you have survived a rape, it is important not to blame yourself, and to take action. If you choose to involve the police or other authorities, it is important to preserve any evidence that can be used to prosecute the rapist. This means not washing away blood, semen, hair, or other substances that could be used to identify your attacker. The authorities will make certain that you are examined and treated by medical personnel, and interviewed about the details of the crime. Although this may be a difficult process for any victim, it can help assure that the rapist is punished.

Many rape victims go through psychological reactions to the trauma. At first, they may be able to put it out of their minds, but eventually they begin to experience anxiety, fear, and depression. They may be upset by feelings of being vulnerable, and fear that they could be raped again. There are rape crisis centers and counselors who can help individuals get through the difficult process of recovering from being raped. It is a process that takes time, but support from counselors and friends can ease the way. Seek help from those who know how to provide appropriate counseling and action.

OTHER FORMS OF SEXUAL EXPLOITATION

Sexual exploitation can take many forms, and sometimes it is not completely clear who is doing the exploiting and who is being exploited. However, it is clear that sex can become part of some questionable connections between human beings, in which the risks of emotional or physical harm are increased. Some examples follow.

Exhibitionism and Voyeurism

Some forms of sexual behavior are exploitative, even though there is no physical contact with the "victim." One is *exhibitionism*. Exhibitionists are people, usually men, who obtain pleasure by exposing their sex organs to other people, usually strangers and usually women or children. Although exhibitionists do not physically harm others, some people may be insulted, frightened, or offended by such behavior. The other behavior is *voyeurism*, refering to the enjoyment that some people get from seeing nude people or people engaged in sexual acts. The voyeur or "peeping Tom" is driven to peek in windows and violating others' privacy by the need for sexual pleasure. There are laws that can lead to the prosecution of exhibitionists and voyeurs.

Many people have mild feelings of exhibitionism. They simply enjoy having their bodies admired, including their sex organs. Many others have feelings of voyeurism. They enjoy seeing others in the nude. But the kinds of exhibitionism and voyeurism we've been discussing are examples of how sexual impulses can become exploitative when they are expressed without regard for the rights and choices of others.

Prostitution

Prostitution refers to paying people for sex. Most prostitutes are women, paid to have sex with men, although some male prostitutes are also available for women. There are homosexual prostitutes too. There are many reasons why people have sexual contact with prostitutes. Regardless of the reason, it is obviously a casual form of sex, with little emotional involvement between the partners. It is primarily a physical experience rather than a total sexual encounter involving feelings and the whole personality.

Studies over the past thirty years have shown that the percentage of young men who have contact with prostitutes has dropped sharply, probably the result of changing sex-related values in our culture.

Of course, there is always the danger of being infected by H.I.V. or some other sexually transmitted disease (STD) from a prostitute. One of the arguments in favor of legalized prostitution is that legalization would permit the government to establish regulations requiring constant STD checks on prostitutes.

Women and men most often become prostitutes because they are desperate for money. It is in this sense that they are being sexually exploited. They find themselves in the unhappy situation of feeling forced to sell their own bodies in order to survive. However, it also can be said that a prostitute's customers are being exploited because they are paying for sex. Either way, in most locations there are laws that prohibit being a prostitute, and also prohibit paying for the services of a prostitute.

Telephone and Computer Sex

There are two ways in which telephones are used for sexual exploitation. *Obscene telephone callers* are people who use the telephone to harass people by making sexually suggestive remarks. Obscene telephone callers may get some degree of arousal from their actions, and may masturbate while making their calls. There is also an element of hostility and violence in their actions. They are exploiting others because they do not identify themselves, intrude into another person's life with upsetting sexual activity, and leave the person they have called feeling upset and confused.

Obscene telephone callers are usually insecure people who have not been able to establish successful relationships with others. If you receive such a call, the best advice is to hang up immediately. Do not try to engage the caller in conversation, and do not encourage the obscene remarks. If obscene phone calls persist, your telephone company will assist in tracing their source, and police will take appropriate action against the caller. Such individuals are rarely dangerous in other ways, but you should not have to be subjected to any sort of sexual harassment over the telephone. Again, take action promptly, and do not allow yourself to be victimized.

A relatively recent development in telephone sex is the availability of sex lines through "900 numbers." People call these numbers in order to listen to someone talking in sexually provocative ways. Some 900 lines offer recorded voices, and some offer the services of real people. Although little research has been done concerning 900 sex lines, they have become a big business. Callers are usually male, and they often are masturbating during the call.

One positive side of this kind of telephone sex is that it is not as risky as many forms of shared sex. On the negative side is the fact that there is a steep charge for such calls. Callers often are exploited financially because the per minute charge for a call is extremely high. Calls are manipulated by the 900 line companies so that you typically will have to spend several minutes on the phone, just reaching the voice that you are looking for. Beyond the financial exploitation, there is the questionable encouragement to share intimacies with an anonymous stranger. For the most part, 900 line telephone sex is probably relatively harmless, unless it becomes a constant need, but it may also represent an unwise and irresponsible use of money.

As people become part of computer networks and "bulletin boards," exploitative sexual communications between anonymous communicators are becoming more common. Again, if you are being subjected to unwelcome sexually suggestive comments via a computer network, seek help from someone who can identify your harasser and put a stop to their actions.

Sexual Addiction?

The topic of sexual addiction was popular for a time on television talk shows and in magazine articles. It has been claimed that for some people, sexual behavior becomes an addiction, much like alcohol or drugs might become. This means that a person has become compulsive about sex, and finds it difficult to regulate his or her sexual behavior. Experts who have promoted the idea of sex addiction insist that for sex addicts, sexual compulsions control their lives, often creating serious problems for themselves and their families.

Other professionals have rejected the idea of sex addiction, saying that there is a danger that people will use the idea of having this "illness" as an excuse for irresponsible and exploitative sexual behavior. We certainly know that for some people, sex becomes exaggeratedly important for their lives. Sometimes, that phase passes rather rapidly. Only time will tell if sex addiction is accepted by professional groups as a true addiction.

If you feel that you are being exploited by your own sexual needs, and that sexual activities are somehow interfering with other aspects of your life, it would be a good idea to seek help from a qualified counselor.

EXAMINING SEXUAL EXPLOITATION

The following activities will help you think through the material that has been covered in this chapter, and figure out how it might be relevant to your life.

Back to the Beginning

Reread the scenarios presented at the beginning of this chapter. What kind of sexual exploitation is represented by each one? What sort of action could each of the victims have taken? The following questions might help in thinking each situation through. Discuss your thoughts and reactions with others, and see what other ideas you come up with.

1. *Jennifer*
   The first time Jennifer was embarrassed by the boys on the bus, what might she have done to assure that their behavior would not be repeated? Why do you think she felt embarrassed?
2. *Jason*
   Do you believe that Jason was being sexually harassed? Why or why not? He was in a very tough situation, and it may have seemed to him that there was nothing he could do without potentially making the situation even worse. If Jason were your friend, and obviously upset by the incident, what would you recommend to him?
3. *Anna*
   Why does Anna's situation so clearly represent sexual harassment? What risks would she take by proceeding with some sort of complaint to the manager who was bothering her, or

to someone else about him? What risks is she taking by not letting anyone know that she is upset? What do you think Anna ought to do?

4. *Tim*

   What parts of this scenario bother you the most, and why? Would it make a difference to you if one of the people in the story was a girl? Why? How do you think Tim should react to Ken's suggestion?

5. *Julie*

   How do you think Julie felt after the incident with her boyfriend? How should she react? From whom should Julie seek help? Do you believe that her boyfriend should be arrested for raping her?

6. *Bob*

   Was Bob subjected to sexual abuse? Why did you give the answer you did? Would you look at this situation any differently if it had involved a fifteen-year-old girl who was fondled by an older uncle? Are there any myths or stereotypes that this scenario suggests? Should Bob have told another adult what happened to him? What would you have done in a similar situation?

7. *Maria*

   What should Maria have done, as soon as she realized what the man in the car was doing? Do you think she should contact the police?

8. *Michael*

   Obviously, Michael's personal situation was a difficult and complicated one. How might he have dealt with the situation at home differently? Instead of becoming a prostitute, what other options could he have? If you were a street social worker, what might you recommend for Michael?

9. *Yvonne*

   What would you do if you received an obscene telephone call as Yvonne did? Do you feel that Yvonne reacted to the situation in the most effective way?

Responding to Sexual Harassment

Think about incidents of sexual harassment that you have experienced yourself or have seen other people experience. They may well include things such as:

> People being grabbed or having their clothing pulled in a sexually aggressive way.

> Having to be exposed to graffiti of an obscene nature, which you find personally offensive, in school hallways or in bathrooms.

> Having another person make insulting remarks about your gender, appearance, or body.

> Being constantly pestered by someone who finds you attractive, even though you have made it clear you're not interested in dating or a closer relationship.

> Being subjected to inappropriate advances or touching from a person who is in an authoritative position over you.

> Having another person tell you dirty jokes that you do not appreciate, or find insulting to yourself or particular groups of people.

Give some thought to how you or your school might address these issues. Investigate whether your school has a policy that specifically prohibits sexual harassment. If it does not, approach the administration of the school or the Student Council with a suggestion that such a policy be developed. Clear sexual harassment policies can make it a lot easier for someone who feels that harassment has taken place to take appropriate action. Don't allow your school to ignore the sexual harassment that takes place there, or to minimize its importance. It is in school that attitudes and values for adult life are supposed to be shaped.

In coming up with an effective sexual harassment policy for a school, there are several things you may want to consider:

Students should be involved in developing the policy.

It should take a clear stand against sexual harassment.

Everyone in the school may need to receive information about what sexual harassment is.

The policy should make it clear what steps can be taken if one is sexually harassed, and offer several different options.

The policy should be put into writing and be well publicized within the school and community.

It should include provisions for follow-up, to assure that there will be no retaliation against any individual who makes a complaint.

Just For You

As you read this chapter, you may have realized — perhaps for the first time — that in some way you have been sexually harassed, abused, or exploited. Even if the incident happened in the past, it is not too late to take whatever action you might need to take in order to deal with your own feelings. It may not even be too late to take action against the person who victimized you.

Some of the organizations listed in Appendix II, on page 255–258, may be able to help you find help in dealing with any sort of sexual exploitation. Remember that you are not alone. Many young people have been subjected to inappropriate sexual treatment. And many have been helped to cope with the confusing mixture of feelings they have experienced. Seek whatever help you need to regain a full sense of control over your own life and emotions.

For Further Reading

Hunter, Michael. *Abused Boys: The Neglected Victims of Child Abuse.* Lexington, Massachusetts: Lexington Books, 1990.

Levy, B. *Dating Violence: Young Women in Danger.* Seattle, Washington: Seal Press, 1991.

Maltz, Wendy. *The Sexual Healing Journey: A Guide for Survivors of Sexual Abuse.* New York: HarperCollins, 1991.

Warshaw, R. *I Never Called it Rape.* New York: HarperCollins, 1988.

11 More Questions and Answers About Sexuality and Relationships

Even after reading the previous chapters in this book, there is a good chance you will still have some questions about human sexuality. New questions come to my mind often, and I sometimes have to search for a book or a person who can answer them.

In this chapter, I'll answer some of the questions that young people have often asked me but that are not discussed in detail in other sections of this book. If you have further questions not answered in this chapter, try looking up the topics in the index and finding information in earlier chapters. The references listed at the end of each chapter may also be good sources for further information.

Questions About Personal Values and Sex

Why don't parents talk to their kids more about sex?
There are plenty of reasons. Parents often have difficulty seeing their children as sexual people and prefer to avoid the whole issue. Sometimes, parents put off talking about sex

until they realize that their kids already know quite a a bit about it; then they decide it won't be necessary to talk about sex at all. Some parents are just too embarrassed to deal with sexual topics or feel that they do not have enough information themselves to be able to explain anything well. They may hope that the school will do something with sex education. There are even some adults who say that the less children are told about sex the better, somehow trying to believe that if kids don't learn about sex, they won't have sexual feelings or want to experiment with it. It should be kept in mind, however, that many people believe sex education to be one of the important responsibilities of parenthood. Of course, not dicussing sex is a form of sex education too. It teaches that sex is something mysterious—perhaps even frightening or ugly—which should not be discussed.

How may a person overcome personal shyness toward sex and sexual activities?

Shyness is not necessarily a bad thing, and some other people might find it quite appealing and appropriate. Although we live in times when people discuss sex more openly, boldness and aggressiveness regarding sex is a real turnoff for many. Nearly everyone is afraid and shy when they first start trying to establish loving relationships and when they first begin to explore sex. Often, much of the shyness disappears as confidence is gained. When shyness is considered to be a real problem by the individual, he or she might want to talk about it with a trusted friend or counselor (see Chapter 7). Among high school and college students, shyness is a common complaint.

What has caused sex to be called dirty? Is sex really dirty or is it whatever people wish to make it?

Our sex organs and sexual feelings are simply a part of human life. As civilized people began to realize the responsibilities and problems that go along with sex, rules, morals, and social attitudes began to develop. Different religions and cultures have very different values concerning the rights and wrongs of sexual behavior. The undercurrent of negative attitudes about sex in our culture—thinking of it as "dirty"—is largely the result of attitudes left over from previous periods in our history. The general feeling at that time was that sex should be used only to produce children and that sexual feelings and activity were mostly bad and disgusting. People were encouraged to deny and control their sexual feelings, often creating great guilt and conflict. Attitudes today are taking a less restrictive view of sex. However, more open sexual attitudes place more of the responsibility for careful decision-making on each of us as individuals.

Is it normal to feel and act sexually the way I do?
This is a question that people have been asking for a long time. I try to keep two major points in mind: that values concerning sexual "normalcy" are determined by one's society, and that no one really knows how we get to be the highly individualized sexual beings that we each become. Because there is really such a wide range of orientations, feelings, needs, and behaviors that human beings exhibit, I don't think it makes sense to focus on issues of "normalcy." Instead, we need to concentrate on understanding and accepting who we are as sexual individuals, with an emphasis on being responsible and nonhurtful to ourselves and others.

We always hear about boys trying to be seducers. Do girls ever set out to seduce?
Seduction refers to an attempt at enticing a person into sexual activity. If one person seduces another through lies or trickery, that is irresponsible and exploitative (See Chapters 5 and 10). If both people are aware of what is happening and want to have sex, then it becomes a mutual seduction, and

that may or may not be a responsible sexual encounter. In any case, seduction is often initiated by both males and females. It is also often done in irresponsible and exploitative ways by both males *and* females.

Questions About the Body and Sex Organs

Is it normal for one of a woman's breasts to be larger than the other?

Many young women worry about their breasts. It is quite common for one breast to be slightly larger than the other. It is also typical for one breast to hang at a different position than the other. The great differences in women's breasts are largely the result of heredity and have nothing to do with how "sexy" a woman is. (See Chapter 2.)

What is a hysterectomy? Can a woman still have sex after she has had a hysterectomy?

A hysterectomy is a surgical procedure in which the woman's uterus is removed. Often, one or both of the ovaries are also removed. This surgery is done for a variety of reasons but especially when abnormal cells are detected indicating that the uterus is the site of a cancerous growth. Many physicians say it is wise for a woman to get the opinion of more than one doctor before agreeing to this surgery. In most hysterectomies, the vagina is not removed, although its position may be slightly different after the surgery. Women can still enjoy a full range of sexual activities following a hysterectomy, including intercourse. Of course, pregnancy is not a possibility after removal of the uterus.

What is a Pap Test and what does a doctor do during an internal pelvic examination of a woman?

For a Pap Test, a physician inserts a small instrument into the vagina and painlessly extracts some fluid and cells from the area of the cervix. A smear is made of this material on a glass slide and it is stained. Then, a trained specialist examines the smear under a microscope, looking for any abnormal cells that might indicate the beginning of disease, especially cancer. Girls and women should consider the Pap Test an essential part of regular physical examinations. For an internal, or pelvic examination, a physician inserts two fingers into the vagina, using surgical gloves and a lubricant. By pushing gently against the uterus with these fingers and placing the other hand on the woman's abdomen, the physician can detect some abnormalities in shape or size of the uterus and ovaries. Some women worry that they will become sexually aroused by such an examination, but their worries are unfounded.

Is an erection of the penis caused by the testes or by the mind?
The testes produce male hormones that may have a minor effect on the male's interests and arousability for sex. The actual mechanism of penis erection is controlled largely by a spinal reflex. However, the mind (brain's cerebral cortex) has input too. Thinking about sex can stimulate an erection, just as fear or anxiety can make erection difficult. In men whose spinal cords have been severed so that there is no connection between the brain and the penis, erection can still occur because of the reflex. Many men who are paralyzed below their waists can still experience erection and participate in sexual activities. (See Chapter 2.)

If a man has lost one testis, can he still have a normal sex life?
In males who have only one testis, there is usually no effect on sexual feelings, sexual performance, or the ability to reproduce. Their bodies develop normally, they are sexually active, and they can produce children.

Is there any way to make a penis larger than it is?
No, nor is there any good reason for trying. A boy's penis

reaches nearly its full growth by his later teenage years, but penis size has nothing to do with the amount of pleasure it can give him or a partner. Some devices are sold with advertising suggesting they might increase penis size. Such devices are ineffective, and may cause damage to the penis. Males' penises are found in a variety of sizes and shapes, all perfectly normal and functional, unless some disease has actually produced an abnormally small organ. (See Chapter 2.)

During a physical examination of a male, why does the doctor feel behind the testes and ask the guy to cough?

Anytime an internal organ pushes through a weakness in the surrounding muscles, it is called a hernia, or rupture. There is a particular kind of hernia in which a small section of intestine may protrude through abdominal muscles and even move down into the scrotum at times. The doctor is pushing at the opening where such a hernia could be felt, and coughing would cause it to be even more evident. This type of hernia is not very common. When present, it may require some sort of medical treatment. Hernias have nothing in particular to do with sex, even though young people joke about them as if they did.

What are "blue balls," and how do you get rid of them?

Sometimes, when a boy is sexually aroused for a long period of time, without ejaculating, the testes and scrotum become somewhat sore. This is the result of having a great deal of blood collecting in the sex organs, resulting in temporary swelling. Having an orgasm is one way to release the pressure and relieve the situation. However, this never should be used as an excuse to have sex with a partner. In fact, some soreness may persist for a brief time even after orgasm. Without orgasm, the soreness gradually will diminish over a few hours. This is not a particularly common condition, and although it may feel uncomfortable, it is not harmful or dangerous.

Questions About Sexual Functioning

At what ages does sex start to interest boys and girls? How old should two people be before they engage in sexual activity?

This varies a great deal with different individuals. Some boys and girls become interested in sex and have sexual feelings at quite young ages, whereas others may not have such interests until they are teenagers or even older. There is also no way of establishing an age when people are ready for sex. Again, that varies with individuals and their circumstances. Each person must decide what kinds of limits he or she wants to have for sexual activities, taking into consideration many factors of responsibility. Careful reading of this book can help you think about some of these factors.

How much sex can you have when you're young without hurting yourself for later on in life? If you have too many orgasms when you're young, will it make you unable to have sex when you're age fifty or older?
Sex and orgasms are not "used up" after a certain limit of activity has been reached. The male body continues to produce semen into old age, and both women and men can still have orgasms when they are old. As a matter of fact, research shows that the more sexually active a person is in youth and middle age, the more active he or she will tend to be in older age. Different people differ in how often they desire sexual release, and their bodies adjust themselves to those needs, regardless of age.

Do boys get sexually excited easier than girls?
There is a great deal of controversy over this very question

today. Traditionally, it had been assumed that boys become sexually aroused more quickly than girls and that boys' sexual interests were stronger. Current research is indicating that this is probably not true at all. Although sexual excitement in boys may be more noticeable because of erection of the penis, girls have the potential of becoming aroused just as rapidly and to as great an extent. It is certainly not true either that a girl can be expected to be in greater control of her sexual feelings and therefore should be the one to stop a sexual encounter before it "goes too far."

I'm a girl, and I don't understand how an erect penis can ever fit into a vagina. Isn't the vagina too small?
Many girls worry that a penis will never be able to fit into their vaginas. Actually, the walls of the vagina are very elastic and can accommodate even a very thick penis. (After all, the vagina can stretch to allow a large baby to be born.) During sexual excitement the vagina lengthens and widens somewhat, and the inner walls become slippery with lubrication. These changes help with accommodation of the penis. During early sexual contacts, plenty of time should be taken for insertion of the penis, to avoid any discomfort and to allow for proper lubrication. (See Chapter 2.)

Why is it that a male sometimes can't keep his erection during sexual activity?
When a male has difficulty maintaining the erection of his penis, professionals usually refer to the problem as *impotence.* Most males experience erection difficulties from time to time, often the result of fatigue, nervousness, depression, alcohol or drug consumption, or just not being especially excited sexually. It may be a signal of guilt about sex or some feelings that need to be talked over with his partner. Some men have trouble getting an erection when they feel pressured to perform well in sex and have some fear that they will

not meet expectations. Occasional problems of this sort are best dealt with by accepting them without embarrassment or fear. If a problem remains for a long period of time, it may be wise to seek help from a qualified sex therapist. (See Chapter 7.)

How long does it take for an average person to reach an orgasm?
The length of time required to reach orgasm varies with the individual and the amount of stimulation. During sexual activity, the majority of men reach orgasm four minutes after entering the vagina. Some men may reach orgasm in a minute or less. However, it is possible for males to *learn* how to prolong the time it takes to reach orgasm, especially by careful attention to masturbating slowly and not allowing oneself to ejaculate. Yet, again there is much individual variation. Some women can reach orgasm a few seconds after beginning intense sexual activity; others might require a much longer time and more direct stimulation of the clitoris. (See Chapter 3.)

Why is it that people sometimes feel guilty after having sex?
People feel guilty whenever they do something that they think is wrong or that has hurt someone. When a sexual encounter leads to guilt, it may be the result of having learned that sex is wrong or bad in some way. It may also mean that before the individual engages in sexual activity again, he or she should think about it carefully and talk seriously about sex with others. Several exercises at the ends of chapters in this book may be able to help you think through your attitudes and values about sex.

Can a doctor tell by any kind of examination whether or not you have had sexual activity?
Generally speaking, no. There is no way of determining what

kinds of sexual activities are being participated in by examining the penis, mouth, or throat. In the vagina and anus, the presence of sperm in a microscopic examination is an indication of sexual activity, but such as examination must take place within a few hours. Presence or absence of the hymen, is, of course, not an accurate indication. Presence of a sexually transmitted disease is a sign that some sort of sexual contact has taken place for both males and females.

How do you know if you're ready to have sex?
This may be one of the most difficult questions to answer, because it depends so much on individual characteristics such as maturity, communication skills, and many other factors. Plenty of people who think they are ready for sex end up regretting their sexual experiences. So there are no surefire guidelines here. However, I believe there are several issues worth considering. You are not ready for sex until you can think through all of the possible consequences, including the emotional ones; until you can talk together as partners about the experience; until you can be sure you are preventing an unintended pregnancy or transmission of a disease; and until you can feel that it is the right thing for you and your partner. Some of the exercises in other chapters of this book, such as those in Chapter 5, may help you to think through your answer to this question more thoroughly.

How can I be the best possible sexual partner?
By knowing how to communicate about sex, and everything else, with sensitivity, honesty, and a sense of consideration. By asking what your partner would like to do; letting your partner know what you want to do; and respecting their wishes as well as your own. By not worrying about how well you are performing, and paying attention instead to relaxing and enjoying yourselves. By being responsible for your own sexual enjoyment while being responsive to your partner. By making certain you are both being safely sexual.

Questions About Relationships

How do I know when it's sexual harassment?
With heightened awareness of sexual harassment and abuse, people of both sexes are facing their personal confusion and misunderstandings about these issues. Many people are realizing for the first time that they have been subjected to harassment or abuse in the past. Others are realizing that their past behaviors may well have been harassing or abusive to others. If you have been touched or talked to in ways that were sexually suggestive and unwanted by you, then it was harassing. Your first responsibility is to protect yourself and to let the offender know that you do not welcome the behavior. Beyond that, you may want to seek help and protection from appropriate authorities. On the other side of the coin, it is best not to touch, talk to, or joke with other people in ways that might be perceived as sexually inappropriate or offensive. The best practice is to ask someone what they consider acceptable and appropriate before acting. All of us must take responsibility for preventing and dealing with sexual harassment and abuse. That means being careful not to let it happen in the first place, stopping it quickly so it doesn't go any farther, and not letting it go by without comment or action once it has happened.

How can I keep the person I love from leaving me?
A healthy loving relationship grows from a mutual commitment on the part of both people. We cannot make another person love us or want to stay with us. In the long run, we cannot change ourselves to give them exactly what they want. When your partner wants to end the relationship, and you don't, it can hurt a great deal. It could be a good time to consider counseling for yourself or for the two of you. In the end, though, you will need to find your ways of letting go, dealing with your hurt feelings, and staying open to new relationships in the future.

How will I know when I've found the partner who will be right to spend the rest of my life with?

Our society has created some curious romantic expectations about finding that Mr. or Ms. Right who is waiting out there for us. It also has led us to believe that you eventually will fall in love with someone, and that you'll know when "it's forever." Like it or not, the process of falling in love eventually ends for everyone. If that process is not replaced by a deeper commitment to working together at keeping the relationship considerate, caring, and genuine on a day-to-day basis, the relationship is probably doomed. A good relationship is not predetermined at the time of meeting your partner; it emerges out of the work you do together to communicate, to resolve differences, to keep up with your changing sexual needs over time, and to give one another room and encouragement to grow. More than finding that one right person for your life, it is working together with the person you have chosen to be with to make the relationship the best it can be for the both of you.

Questions About Other Sexual Activities

Can a person go through life without any sex and still be happy? If you don't masturbate or have sexual intercourse, can you become physically ill?

Having sexual feelings and needing to express them are important and normal parts of the human personality. Very few people go through life without having at least some outlets for their sexual drives. No physical damage is done by not participating in sexual activities. However, if lack of participation in sex results from fear, guilt, other negative attitudes about one's own sexuality, or inability to become involved with other people, emotional difficulties may develop that might require some discussion with a good counselor. (See Chapter 7.)

Can masturbation cause any damage to physical or mental health?

Masturbation is a harmless practice, not leading to any physical or mental damage. Medically speaking, there's no such thing as "too much" masturbation. However, once might be too much if you think that it is wrong for you. Masturbation is a normal way of expressing sexual feelings, and almost everyone masturbates at various time during his or her life. Of course, it is also all right to choose not to masturbate. (See Chapter 3.)

Can I be sure I'm not gay?

In recent years, experts in the field of human sexuality have been trying to get beyond the old labels and assumptions that have dominated our thinking about sexual orientation. It is just too simplistic to categorize people as either gay or straight. The best evidence would suggest that sexual orientation is not something that is either-or. Instead, it seems to be a conglomeration of sexual fantasies, attractions, relationships, feelings, perceptions, and choices of behaviors that may shift and change with time and circumstances. This is not to say that you might wake up some morning with a whole new sexual orientation. Most people know inside what their main sexual orientations are. The sexual choices they make, however, may be influenced by a variety of things. The sooner we stop worrying about who is gay and who is straight, or making assumptions about who is better than someone else because of sexual attractions, the better off we'll all be.

Questions About Miscellaneous Sex Facts

Is there such a thing as "Spanish Fly" and does it really get you sexually turned on? Do any foods or drugs enhance sexual performance?

"Spanish Fly" is the slang name for cantharides, a chemical extracted from a European beetle that has been rumored to make people sexually excited. It is often talked about as a substance that is slipped into a person's drink or food so they will be easier to persuade into sex later, which is obviously an irresponsible, exploitative attitude. In fact, cantharides does not increase sexual desire and can be a dangerous chemical to take into the body, with serious—even deadly—side effects. Certain foods (olives, eggs) and drugs have also developed reputations as being aphrodisiacs—sexual stimulants. These are apparently myths. Although certain drugs, such as alcohol and marijuana, may lower sexual inhibitions, they apparently often hinder actual sexual performance.

What is the best form of birth control?
Anybody can look up the statistics on contraceptive effectiveness, and this information can provide one useful guideline for making a choice about a method to use. However, there are other factors to be considered, and any method should be consistent with the life-styles and preferences of both partners. Here are some other issues to consider in choosing a birth control method for your relationship: Can you afford it? Is it a method you will be motivated to use properly every time? Does it provide the degree of protection that is reasonable for your frequency of intercourse? Does it provide protection from disease if that is a potential consideration for you and your partner? What are its side effects and potential risks? The best way to select a form of contraception is to talk over the choices with an expert who can help you get all the information you need. Most birth control clinics are well prepared to do just that.

Can doctors tell before a baby is born whether it is a boy or a girl?
Several tests have been developed to determine the sex of a child before birth, but most are not considered reliable. One

method that can be used, but is generally not done unless there is a special medical problem, is examination of amniotic fluid. A long, hollow needle is inserted through the pregnant woman's abdomen into the amnion surrounding the fetus, and a small amount of fluid is withdrawn containing some cells from the fetus. Special techniques are then used to make the chromosomes in these cells visible. At that time the sex chromosomes can be observed and a determination made as to whether they are XX (a girl) or XY (a boy). Most physicians make no attempt to determine the sex of a child until it is born. (See Chapter 9.)

Questions About STD and H.I.V. Infection

How can I be sexual and still be safe from AIDS?
The danger of infection by the human immunodeficiency virus (H.I.V.) certainly has added an entirely new dimension to sex for the present generation of young people. I am always heartened when teenagers are informed enough to be concerned about the risks. I like to emphasize that we can use this crisis to offer some fresh perspectives on sex. For example, abstinence from shared sex now represents a very rational and sensible choice. However, it will not be the only choice that young adults make. We also can remember that sexual sharing can mean far more than sexual intercourse or other forms of penetrative sex. Kissing, embracing, and cuddling can be very romantic and satisfying. There are plenty of enjoyable sexual activities that are relatively low in risk, and for the riskier activities, latex condoms offer a great deal of protection. Condoms are not completely risk-free, but they are far safer than unprotected sex.

How can I know for sure when it is safe to have sex with a person I really love, without using a condom?
This is going to be one of the most difficult issues for this generation to resolve, and there are not always going to be

easy answers. Medical science has generally suggested that H.I.V. antibodies will show up in blood tests within six months after infection, and that is still believed to be a reasonably reliable guideline. However, there is now evidence that some people have developed AIDS without previously testing positive for H.I.V., a very disturbing possibility. More than ever before, developing an honest and trusting relationship with a loving partner is crucial. If either partner has risked infection with previous sexual partners, it will be essential to wait at least six months before being tested for H.I.V. antibodies, and then it might be advisable to wait even longer before having unprotected sex and follow-up tests. These limitations are bound to place very real pressures on relationships, but can also provide opportunities for the relationship to grow and deepen.

Can you get an STD from dirty hands?
No. You get sexually transmitted diseases (STD) when a germ is transmitted to your body by an infected person, regardless of her or his degree of cleanliness or yours. Because STD germs can survive outside the body for only a very few seconds, they are almost always transmitted by direct body contact, especially when the sex organs are together. Cleanliness is no guarantee of protection against STDs. (See Chapter 8.)

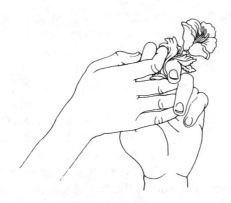

Appendix I: The Words We Use: A Glossary

Here is an alphabetical list of words that relate to human sexuality. For some of the words, proper pronunciation is given.

More information on most terms may be found by consulting the index and finding the pages in the text where the words are used.

Abortion—the expulsion of an embyro or fetus from the uterus before birth.

Abstinence—choosing not to participate in sexual activity.

Acquaintance rape—being forced into sexual activity by someone who is known to you.

Adolescence—a time of growth and changes between childhood and adulthood.

AIDS—an acronym for acquired immunodeficiency syndrome, a serious disease that can be transmitted through sexual contact. It is the final stages of H.I.V. disease.

Artificial insemination—placing a male's sperm in a woman's vagina with medical instruments, to increase the chances that pregnancy will occur.

Bisexual—a person who is sexually attracted by and/or participates in sexual activity with members of both sexes.

Cervix (SIR-vicks)—the narrow part of the female's uterus, or neck
of the uterus, which extends into the vagina.

Chancre (SHANK-er)—a painless, oozing sore that appears in early
syphilis, usually on the sex organs.

Chlamydia (kla-MID-ee-uh)—a sexually transmitted disease that
has become a national epidemic. It often creates only mild
symptoms, but should be treated promptly.

Circumcision (sir-come-SIZ-zhun)—removal of the foreskin, or
fold of skin that covers the end of the boy's penis.

Climax—see orgasm.

Clitoris (KLIT-or-iss)—a small organ located above the opening of
the vagina in the female vulva; highly sensitive to sexual
stimulation.

Cohabitation—living together without being married; a sexual
relationship usually is implied by the term.

Coitus (KOH-ih-tuss)—a scientific term for sexual intercourse.

Coming out—letting other people know that you have a homosexual orientation; "coming out of the closet."

Conception (kun-SEP-shun)—see fertilization.

Condom (KON-dum)—a rubber or membrane sheath worn over
the penis during sexual intercourse to collect semen, prevent
pregnancy, and prevent the spread of sexually transmitted
diseases.

Contraceptive (kon-tra-SEP-tiv)—any device that prevents fertilization of an ovum by a sperm.

Crabs—slang term for sexually transmitted pubic lice that infect
the pubic area, causing itching. They are highly contagious.

Cunnilingus—oral sex performed on a female.

Diaphragm (DI-uh-fram)—a rubber disk inserted into the vagina
and over the cervix before intercourse to prevent sperm from
entering the uterus. It is used with a spermicidal jelly.

Egg—see ovum.

Ejaculation (ee-jack-u-LAY-shun) — the sudden emission of semen from the penis during male orgasm.

Embryo (EHM-bree-oh) — a developing organism. For the first 8 weeks of development in the uterus, the developing fertilized egg may be called an embryo.

Erection (ee-RECK-shun) — the male's penis becoming filled with blood, so that it becomes longer, thicker, harder, and stiffer.

Erotic (ee-ROT-ick) — anything having to do with sexual love and sexual feelings.

Exhibitionist — an individual who gains sexual excitement from exposing the sex organs.

Fallopian tube (fah-LOPE-ee-an) — a hollow tube leading from the ovaries to the uterus. Fertilization usually takes place while the ovum is in this tube.

Fellatio — oral sex performed on a male.

Feminist — person who believes in the equality of women and men and advocates equal treatment of the sexes in jobs, laws, and other aspects of society.

Femininity — personality factors and behaviors that we tend to associate with being female.

Fertilization — a sperm entering an ovum, combining the chromosomes.

Fetus (FEE-tuss) — the developing infant inside the female's uterus from about 8 weeks until birth.

Flasher — a common name for an exhibitionist, someone who exposes sex organs to others for sexual pleasure.

Foreplay — sexual activity that eventually leads to more intensive sexual activity such as intercourse.

Foreskin — the fold of skin that covers the head of the boy's penis at birth. The head, or glans penis, is exposed by pulling the foreskin back.

Gay — slang for homosexual or bisexual; preferred by most homosexual men, whereas most homosexual women prefer to be called "lesbians."

Gender identity—our inner sense of our own maleness and femaleness, masculinity and femininity; how we see ourselves as a woman or a man.

Gonad—biological term for a sex gland, either ovaries or testes.

Gonorrhea (gone-or-REE-uh)—a sexually transmitted disease often characterized by a burning feeling during urination and discharge of pus from the urethra.

Herpes (HER-peez)—a viral sexually transmitted disease characterized by painful blisters that may recur.

Heterosexual—anything applying to the opposite sex.

Hickey—a black and blue mark, often on the neck, caused by vigorous sucking on the skin.

H.I.V.—abbreviation for human immunodeficiency virus, the virus that may be transmitted by sexual contact and eventually can lead to AIDS.

Homophobia—unreasonable negative attitudes toward or fears about people who have a homosexual orientation.

Homosexual—anything applying to the same sex. More specifically, an individual who is sexually attracted primarily to others of his or her own sex.

Hormones—chemicals produced by endocrine glands (including the ovaries and testes) that help regulate body activities.

Hymen (HI-mun)—the fold of skin that often partially covers the opening to the vagina in girls, until it has been broken or removed in some way.

Impotence (IM-poh-tense)—inability in a male to achieve or maintain an erection for sexual activity.

Incest—sexual activity between closely related individuals.

Infatuation—the excitement of falling in love with another person and feeling strongly attracted to that person.

Infertility—the inability to conceive and create a pregnancy.

Intercourse—see sexual intercourse.

IUD (or Intrauterine Device)—a birth control device inserted into the woman's uterus to prevent pregnancy.

In vitro fertilization (IVF) — a reproductive technology that involves removal of an egg directly from the ovary, and then fertilizing the egg with sperm in a laboratory. The fertilized egg is then placed in a woman's uterus in hopes that it will implant and develop into an embryo.

Labia (LAY-bee-uh) — the "lips" in the female's vulva area that cover the opening to the vagina.

Lesbian (LEZ-bee-un) — another term for a woman who has a mostly homosexual orientation.

Mammogram — a sensitive x-ray of the female breast that can show possible malignant growths at very early stages.

Masculinity — personality factors and behaviors that we tend to associate with being male.

Masturbation (mass-ter-BAY-shun) — stimulating one's own sex organs, often with the hands, to produce sexual excitement and often orgasm.

Menopause — the time in a woman's life when she has completely stopped having menstrual periods.

Menstruation (men-stroo-AY-shun) — the stage of the female menstrual cycle in which some inner lining of the uterus, along with a small amount of blood, leaves the body through the vagina.

Mons (mahnz) — the small mound of tissue, covered with hair in adults, just above the sex organs.

Natural Family Planning/Fertility Awareness — an approach to birth control that combines charting the menstrual cycle, daily temperature checks, and regular checking of the woman's cervical mucus. If carefully and consistently used, it is an effective strategy for birth control or for determining the best time to get pregnant.

Nocturnal emission — ejaculation of semen from a male's penis while he is asleep.

Norplant implants — a contraceptive that consists of silicone rubber rods that are implanted under the skin of a woman's arm, where they release a hormone into the body that prevents ovulation for up to 5 years.

Orgasm (OR-gaz-um) — the pleasurable release of tension after it has built up as sexual excitement.

Ovary — two glands in the female, located near the uterus, that produce female hormones and ova.

Oviduct — see fallopian tube.

Ovulation (oh-view-LAY-shun) — the time during the female's menstrual cycle when the ovum ruptures through the ovary wall and begins its journey to the fallopian tube.

Ovum (plural; ova) — the egg, produced by the female, which when fertilized by a male's sperm develops into a fetus.

Penis (PEE-niss) — a sex organ of the male, which becomes erect during sexual excitement. It carries both urine and semen to the outside of the male's body.

Pornography — pictures or written material of a sexual nature, which stimulate thinking about sex and sexual arousal.

Possessiveness — an unreasonable level of jealousy about and dependency on a loved one.

Premature ejaculation — a difficulty in which the male reaches orgasm too soon for either his or his partner's enjoyment; also called lack of ejaculatory control.

Prepuce (PREE-poose) — another scientific term for foreskin.

Prostitute — an individual who participates in sexual activity for money.

Puberty — the time in a person's life when the sex organs become capable of reproduction.

Pubic hair (PYOU-bick) — the coarse, curly hair that surrounds the sex organs in older adolescence and adulthood.

Rape — forcing a person to participate in sexual activity against her or his will.

Rubber — slang for condom.

Sado-masochist (SAY-do-MASS-oh-kist) — an individual who gains sexual pleasure by inflicting or receiving pain or humiliation.

Sanitary pad — an absorbent pad used by females to absorb the menstrual flow during menstruation.

Scrotum — the pouch of skin in which the male's testes are contained, below the penis.

Semen (SEE-men) — the thick, sticky fluid that contains sperm, ejaculated by the male from the penis during orgasm.

Sexual abuse — a general term for inappropriate and exploitative sexual behavior, often inflicted on a child by someone older.

Sexual harassment — being subjected to suggestive talk, touch, jokes, or looks that are unwanted, even after telling the offender to stop.

Sexual individuality — the set of sexual interests, needs, feelings, fantasies, and preferences unique to each person.

Sexual intercourse — the erect penis of the male entering the vagina of the female.

Sexually Transmitted Diseases (STD) — those infections whose germs are spread from person to person by close body contact, usually sexual.

Sexual orientation — a person's basic inclinations in sexual interest.

Sperm — the microscopic cells produced by the male's testes that can fertilize the female's ovum.

Sterilization — any procedure that causes a male or female to be unable to reproduce by not allowing the sperm or egg to be present for fertilization.

Straight — a slang term for a heterosexual person.

Surrogate mother — a woman who is paid to carry a pregnancy, with the understanding that she will give the baby to another couple after birth. The pregnancy may be the result of either artificial insemination or in vitro fertilization.

Syphilis (SIFF-ill-is) — a dangerous sexually transmitted disease characterized by three stages.

Tampon — a cylinder of absorbent material inserted into the vagina to absorb the menstrual flow during menstruation.

Testes (TESS-teez) (Singular: testis) — two glands in the male, located in the scrotum, that produce male hormones and sperm.

Transsexual — an individual who feels trapped in a body of the wrong sex, and strongly wants to have a body of the opposite sex.

Transvestite — a person who gets sexual or other gratification from dressing in clothes usually worn by members of the opposite sex.

Tubal ligation — a sterilization procedure in which a woman's fallopian tubes are tied, thus preventing sperm from being able to reach the egg.

Umbilical cord — the cord that attaches a developing fetus to the placenta, transferring food and oxygen to the fetus and waste products to the placenta.

Uterus (YOU-ter-us) — the female reproductive organ in which the fertilized ovum becomes implanted and grows for nine months into a baby.

Vagina (vuh-GINE-uh) — the flexible muscular canal extending down from the uterus to an opening in the vulva. It becomes lubricated during sexual arousal.

Vasectomy — a surgical procedure in which a male's sperm ducts (vas deferens) are cut, rendering him sterile.

Venereal Diseases (vehn-IHR-ee-al) (VD) — several diseases that are transmitted by close body contact, usually sexual; now usually called sexually transmitted diseases (STD).

Virgin — a person who has never experienced sexual intercourse.

Voyeur — an individual who seeks sexual excitement by peeking in windows or other means to see people nude or involved in sex.

Vulva — the external sex organs of the female.

Wet dream — slang for nocturnal emission.

Womb (woom) — another name for the uterus.

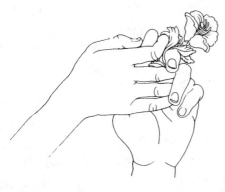

Appendix II:

Organizations Providing Information and Help

About Sexuality, Sex Education, and Family Life

Sex Information and Education Council of the United
    States (SIECUS)
130 West 42nd Street, Suite 2500
New York, New York 10036
Telephone: (212) 819-9770

American Association of Sex Educators, Counselors, and
    Therapists (AASECT)
435 North Michigan Avenue, Suite 1717
Chicago, Illinois 60611
Telephone: (312) 644-0828

Los Angeles Sex Information Helpline
(Telephone information during evening hours Monday–
    Thursday)
Telephone: (213) 653-1123

Kinsey Institute for Sex Research, Inc.
Morrison Hall
Indiana University
Bloomington, Indiana 47405

About Birth Control and Family Planning

Your local Planned Parenthood or Family Planning Agency
(see your telephone directory and local advertising)

Planned Parenthood Federation of America, Inc.
810 7th Avenue
New York, New York 10019
Telephone: (212) 541-7800
  (Can provide a list of local Planned Parenthood
  affiliates.)

The Center for Population Options
1025 Vermont Avenue, N.W., Suite 210
Washington, DC 20005
Telephone: (202) 347-5700

About Sexually Transmitted Diseases

National STD Hotline
National toll-free telephone (for anywhere in U.S.A.):
1 (800) 227-8922
Call for STD information or referral to local clinics for
  treatment. Hours: 8 A.M.–11 P.M. (EST) weekdays.

About Homosexuality and Bisexuality

Bisexual Information and Counseling Service
599 West End Avenue, Suite 1-A
New York, New York 10024
Telephone: (212) 496-9500

National Gay and Lesbian Task Force
1734 14th Street, N.W.
Washington, DC 20009-4309
Telephone: (202) 332-6483

Lesbian and Gay Youth Helpline
(Telephone counseling and advice, Monday and
     Wednesday, 7–10 P.M. Saturday, 3:30–6:30 P.M., EST)
(202) 483-9585

National Gay and Lesbian Crisis Line
1 (800) 221-7044

About H.I.V. and AIDS

AIDS Action Council
729 8th Street, S.E., Suite 200
Washington, DC 20003

AIDS Information
U.S. Public Health Service
Office of Public Affairs, Room 721-H
200 Independence Avenue, S.W.
Washington, DC 20201

AIDS Crisis Line: 1 (800) 221-7044

National AIDS Hotline: 1 (800) 342-AIDS

About Finding Help for Sexual Abuse

The National Child Abuse Hotline and Referral Service:
1 (800) 422-4453

National Center on Child Abuse and Neglect
P.O. Box 1182
Washington, DC 20013
Telephone: (202) 245-2858

Incest Survivors Anonymous
P.O. Box 21817
Baltimore, Maryland 21222
Telephone: (301) 282-3400

ABOUT THE AUTHOR

Gary F. Kelly has been working with young people throughout his professional career as an educator and counselor. He is Headmaster of The Clarkson School and Associate Dean of Students at Clarkson University in Potsdam, New York. He is also a lecturer in the graduate program in Counseling and Human Development at St. Lawrence University. He is certified as a Sex Educator and as a Sex Therapist by the American Association of Sex Educators, Counselors, and Therapists. He is a Diplomate of the American Board of Sexology, and a Clinical Fellow of the American Academy of Clinical Sexologists. He served as Editor of the *Journal of Sex Education and Therapy* from 1982 until 1990. Kelly is a frequent consultant and conference speaker in the field of human sexuality. In addition to this book, he has authored a popular college textbook on sexuality, a book on male sexuality, and numerous articles for professional journals. He lives outside of Potsdam, New York with his wife Betsy and two daughters, Casey and Chelsea.

Index